IN THE LATTER DAYS

In the Latter Days

*The Outpouring of the Holy Spirit
in the Twentieth Century*

Vinson Synan

SERVANT BOOKS
Ann Arbor, Michigan

To the men I had the honor of working with in planning and leading the 1977 Kansas City Charismatic conference: Brick Bradford, Larry Christenson, Ithiel Clemmons, Howard Courtney, Robert Frost, Roy Lamberth, Nelson Litwiller, Bob Mumford, Ken Pagard, Kevin Ranaghan, Carleton Spencer, David Stern, and Ross Whetstone.

Copyright © 1984 by Vinson Synan

Cover photo by Ed Cooper
Book design by John B. Leidy

Available from Servant Publications, Box 8617,
   Ann Arbor, Michigan 48107

ISBN 0-89283-191-X
Printed in the United States of America

84 85 86 87 88 89 10 9 8 7 6 5 4 3 2 1

Library of Congress Cataloging in Publication Data

Synan, Vinson.
   In the latter days.

   Bibliography: p.
   Includes index.
   1. Pentecostalism—History. I. Title.
BR1644.S96 1984   270.8'2   84-14082
ISBN 0-89283-191-X

Contents

Acknowledgments

THE BASIC WORK for *In the Latter Days* was done in 1974 when I was invited to give the King Memorial Lectures at Emmanuel College in Franklin Springs, Georgia where I was teaching at the time. My father, Bishop J.A. Synan, was scheduled to give the lectures that year, but because of a serious eye operation, he was unable to fulfill the appointment. The committee asked me to present the lectures in my father's place.

I felt in 1974 that it was a bit too early to publish a historical treatment of the charismatic movement because the movement was in its formative stages. After ten years, I feel that now is an opportune time to present this study.

The reader will immediately see that this is a popular treatment of the story. I have made no attempt to present this book as an exhaustive or definitive history of the movement. I have tried to present as best I can the major background developments of the nineteenth century which led to the appearance of Pentecostalism in the twentieth century. I have attempted only to describe the beginnings of crucial phases of the movement after 1900.

My major viewpoint is that there is only one outpouring of the Holy Spirit in the latter days, although the streams flow through channels known as "classical pentecostalism," Protestant "neo-Pentecostalism," and the "Catholic charismatic renewal." In the end it adds up to one great historical phenomenon which has had a profound effect on Christianity around the world.

I wish first to acknowledge the encouragement of Martin Marty, Jim Manney, and Bert Ghezzi who all suggested that I write this book. The help of the staff of Servant Publications aided me greatly in all stages of preparing the manuscript.

I hereby thank my faithful office staff who allowed me to discuss historical matters during coffee breaks. Joe Iaquinta, Marcia Matthews, and Esme Coronado were helpful, long-suffering and kind.

Special thanks are also hereby given to my wife, Carol Lee, and my children; Mary, Virginia, Vince, and Joey, who allowed me to hide away at my desk working on the manuscript during the evenings and week-ends when I should have been helping around the house.

I also salute my new companion, the marvelous Kaypro 10 computer and word processor without which this book would not exist. Special thanks also to Joe Barton of PCS computers who helped me greatly with the technical aspects of composing on a word processor. For the first time in my life, I have typewritten a book by myself with my wife and secretaries not having to type a single word.

VINSON SYNAN
Oklahoma City
July 1984

ONE

The Latter Rain

WHAT IN THE WORLD IS GOD DOING? Lately, this question has been increasingly on the minds of Christians, as they have seen the forces of evil come more and more out into the open. How can God permit the mass murder of millions of infants through abortion? How can sexual perversion be so openly flaunted in the nation's media? How can God allow poverty, war, hunger, and mass injustice to afflict huge masses of the earth's population? What on earth is God doing about the onrushing nuclear arms race that threatens to engulf the world in sudden atomic disaster? Why doesn't God intervene in a sudden act of righteous fury to correct the sorry mess our world is in?

Surely, all thinking Christians have wrestled with these questions while reading the newspapers and watching the news. The daily litany of murders, rapes, robberies, wars, and rumors of wars is enough to make one question if God really is in control. For some, even whether he cares about his creation.

On the other hand, there is news of a great resurgence of faith and religion from these same media sources. Christian books sell millions of copies, while churches are building huge, expensive new sanctuaries across the nation. On television, entire networks devoted to bringing the message of Jesus Christ to the world are flourishing. Opinion polls indicate an upsurge in belief and interest in religion, especially among the young people of the nation. What on earth is happening?

The Two Revivals

The scriptures indicate that, in the last days, there will be two revivals taking place at the same time—Satan's revival and God's revival—in one last great struggle to win the allegiance of the people of the world. Why there would be *two* revivals is a question that has puzzled students of biblical prophecy for centuries. Nevertheless, the Bible does seem to say this will happen.

Many scriptures indicate a great apostasy and "falling away" of the saints before the end of the age. In 2 Thessalonians 2:3-4, Paul speaks of a "lawless one" who will be revealed as the enemy, who will claim to be greater than God, and who will enthrone himself in God's sanctuary. This antichrist will deceive millions with a show of signs and wonders, false miracles to convince even church people that he is the Christ.

In his last letter, Paul gives a final warning about the situation at the end of the age (2 Tm 3:1-5):

> You may be sure that in the last days there are going to be some difficult times. People will be self-centered and grasping; boastful, arrogant and rude; disobedient to parents, ungrateful, irreligious; heartless and unappeasable; they will be slanderers, profligates, savages and enemies of everything that is good; they will be treacherous and reckless and demented by pride, preferring their own pleasure to God. They will keep up an outward appearance of religion but will have rejected the inner power of it. Have nothing to do with people like that.

Other scriptures that deal with the terrible apostasy of the end times are found in Matthew 7, 1 Timothy 4, 2 Peter 2, Jude, and Revelation 17. These scriptures point to a period in church history in which spiritual leadership will be taken over by persons who are opposed to everything that Christ and his church have ever stood for. Leading in this satanic revival will be the "unholy trinity" made up of the Beast, the False Prophet, and the Anti-christ. These evil personalities are spoken of in Revelation 19:20; 1 John 2:18-19, 4:3; and 2 John 7. They work in unity against the Father, the Son, and the Holy Spirit.

There can be little question that an unprecedented revival of evil is abroad in the world today. Divorces match the number of marriages in most states. Also, more and more couples are choosing to live together without the benefit of marriage. By 1983, more than 1,000,000 couples in the U.S. were living together without marriage.

The gay rights crusade has brought its parades and political campaigns right into the living rooms of the American public. Several denominations are actually ordaining known, practicing homosexuals into the ministry. We have even seen the creation of a gay denomination that openly advocates a homosexual lifestyle for professed Christians.

Every day this satanic revival comes further into the open. The "worship" services are celebrated daily in the bars, theaters, and X-rated movie houses of the nation. Every home is a potential "house church" for the evil rites of this movement. Cable television now brings the whole liturgy of the satanic revival right into the homes of the nation where children and teen-agers are converted, by the millions, into modern pagans. Satan is doing his utmost to destroy this generation.

The Bible says, "where sin abounded, grace did much more abound" (Rom 5:20). What on earth is God doing? Plenty! The same scriptures that speak of apostasy and a revival of evil in the last days also speak of a great outpouring of the Holy Spirit which will far outstrip the work of Satan in the world. While many Christians are huddled in a corner waiting for Jesus to come, millions more are experiencing the greatest spiritual renewal the church has known since the days of the apostles. The Bible teaches that both revivals will take place at the same time, but with grace gaining the ascendancy.

The biblical basis of the end-time revival is found in the prophecy of Joel which Simon Peter repeated on the day of Pentecost (Jl 2:28-29):

> And it shall come to pass afterward, I will pour out my Spirit upon all flesh; and your sons and daughters shall prophesy, your old men shall dream dreams, your young men shall see visions: and also upon the servants and the handmaids in those days will I pour out my Spirit.

When Peter finished his sermon, 3,000 people were added to the church.

Immediately there followed an explosion of the "signs and wonders," gifts of the Holy Spirit which turned Jerusalem upside down. Prophecy was renewed, while miracles of healing and casting out demon spirits authenticated the gospel in the eyes of the world. Because of the demonstrated power of God, Christianity spread over the known world and, within one generation, could boast of converts in the house of Caesar himself. After these mighty years of miracles, the gifts of the Spirit began to fade from the scene, especially after the centuries of persecution ended with the toleration and political acceptance of the church in the world.

As great as this deluge of the Holy Spirit was in the early church, it could in no way fulfill the vision of Joel, who foresaw an outpouring of the Spirit upon "all flesh." Large areas of the world had not been discovered when Peter preached his Pentecost sermon. Out of the 167 million people on the earth at that time, probably only 20 million could have heard the gospel during the first century. The absolute fulfillment of Joel's prophecy had to wait until "all flesh" could be evangelized.

It has only been in the last century that this prophecy could possibly come to pass. All the continents and peoples of the world have now been effectively reached by the message of the gospel. The promises of the Lord's kingdom are indeed universal: "And the glory of the Lord shall be revealed, and all flesh shall see it together"(Is 40:5). Paul echoed this when he said, "Every knee shall bow" and "every tongue confess that Jesus Christ is Lord" (Phil 2:10-11).

The Latter-Rain Covenant

In the early days of the twentieth century, there began a great worldwide outpouring of the Holy Spirit, with a renewal of the gifts of the Spirit in the church. The leading groups in this renewal have been the pentecostal churches and the charismatic movements in the traditional denominations. This has been such a dramatic revival that J. Edwin Orr's volume on Christianity in this century is entitled *The Flaming Tongue.*

As the gifts of healing, tongues, interpretation of tongues, and discernment of spirits began to be experienced after 1901, ministers began to search the scriptures. One of the earliest treatises was by David Wesley Myland. In his 1910 *The Latter Rain Pentecost,* Myland pointed out the other promise of Joel 2, the promise of the "early" and "latter" rains mentioned in verse 23:

> Be glad then, ye children of Zion and rejoice in the LORD your God: for he has given you the early rain moderately, and he will cause to come down for you the rain, the early and the latter rain in the first month.

This promise refers directly to the pattern of rainfall in Palestine, which continues to this day. The Israelites were fearful of leaving Egypt where there was no lack of water due to the annual overflowing of the Nile River. To them, the Lord promised, "I will give you the rain of your land in his due season, the first rain and the latter rain, that you may gather in your corn, and your wine, and your oil" (Dt 11:14).

This promise was a great comfort to Israel since the "early" rain was the seedtime rain which came in the fall of the year (September 15 through November 15) during the planting season for the winter wheat crop. It was absolutely necessary to have a good rain at this time for the seeds to germinate. This rain the Israelites called the *yarah,* or former rain. The "latter" rain came in the spring of the year just before harvest time and was greatly appreciated because without it the crops could not mature for harvest. It came from March 15 to May 15 and was called by the Jews the *malqosh* rain.

When the latter rain was ended, the harvest ensued with great rejoicing since a good crop guaranteed a year free from hunger. This harvest celebration, known by its Greek name *Pentecost,* followed the gathering of the wheat crop. In time, it became the most joyous feast on the Jewish calendar. Singing and dancing filled the land as the people rejoiced at the harvest bounty given by the Lord.

The scriptures also gave a spiritual and prophetic significance to these early and latter rains that goes far beyond the natural rainfall of Palestine. In Hosea we are told that "He shall come as the latter and the early rain" (6:3). In Proverbs we are told that "His favor is as a cloud of the latter rain" (16:15). In Zechariah we are admonished to "ask for rain in the time of the latter rain" (10:1). In the New Testament, the early and latter rains are connected with the promise of the second coming of Christ and the end of the age. James emphasized this when he wrote (5:7-8):

> Therefore be patient, brothers, until the coming of the Lord. See how the farmer waits for the precious fruit of the earth, waiting patiently for it until it receives the early and latter rain. You also be patient. Establish your hearts, for the coming of the Lord is at hand.

This scripture implies that "early and latter" rains must come before the Lord returns. It also carries into our situation everything that the ancient Jewish agricultural calendar implied—working in the fields, rejoicing at the abundant harvest that will precede the coming of the Lord, and being established in the Lord and his Word.

It was Myland's contention that the church was born in the "early rain" outpouring that began on the day of Pentecost, but that an even greater "latter rain" outpouring awaited the church just before the return of the Lord. Since Joel stated that the early rain would be poured out "moderately," then the latter rain would, of necessity, be greater than the first.

Today, there are in the world millions of people who believe that the church is now in the "latter-rain" stage of God's dealing with mankind. They believe that the greatest miracles and victories in the history of the church will come just before the appearing of the Lord. They fervently believe that all the gifts of the Spirit have been restored to the church and that the bride of Christ will be caught up in a shout of victory rather than in a moan of defeat.

These are the "latter-rain people" and they are members of practically every congregation and denomination in Christendom. They constitute the most vital and fastest-growing movement in the church since the days of the Reformation. Who are they? Where did they come from? What do they believe? This book is an attempt to answer these questions.

In order to gain a perspective on this movement which in recent years has been called the "neo-pentecostal" or "charismatic" movement, it will be necessary to glance at the pages of recent history. Only then will it be possible to venture a few answers as to just what in the world God is doing today.

TWO

The Latter-Rain People

THE TWENTIETH CENTURY has been the most important and tumultuous period in the history of mankind—and it is not over yet. On January 1, 1901, the world population was two billion. By mid-century, that figure has swelled to three billion. By 1980, the number stood at the astronomical total of 4,300,000,000 persons. To a biologist, this represents an explosion in the species. To a Christian theologian, however, this represents a vast increase in the number of immortal souls who will one day stand in the last judgment to give account for their lives on earth.

Some anthropologists say that one half of all the human beings that have ever lived are alive at this moment. Others say that a grand total of some seventy billion people have inhabited the earth and that the present population represents less than ten percent of all the human beings in history. In either case, the number of people alive today represents a very large proportion of the entire human race. The chart on the next page will illustrate this.

These figures are or should be of great interest to all who inhabit the planet. The effects of this population explosion are not lost on those engaged in agriculture, since the feeding of these multitudes each year taxes their limits. Those interested in ecology are more and more discouraged by the effects of overpopulation on the environment. World leaders grapple

Table 1

World Population at:

Birth of Christ	*169,700,000*
500 A.D.	*193,400,000*
1000 A.D.	*269,200,000*
1500 A.D.	*425,300,000*
1800 A.D.	*902,600,000*
1900 A.D.	*1,619,000,000*
1980 A.D.	*4,373,900,000*
1985 A.D.	*4,781,100,000*
2000 A.D.	*6,259,600,000*

daily with the complications of governing a world bursting at the seams. Economists create new theories and refine old ones in their attempts to understand the new pressures created by this great mass of people.

In order to protect the wealth they control, the developed nations continue to build huge armories of devastating weapons that could incinerate mankind in just a few minutes. Wars and rumors of wars continue to plague mankind while world leaders desperately attempt to avert world disaster. All the while, these leaders labor under the sure knowledge that by the end of the century the world population will probably double again, and with this increase in population, the problems in managing world affairs will double also.

Adding to the complexity of these staggering problems is the continuing struggle between the Western democracies and the Communist nations for world leadership. Both systems claim to offer the best hope of leading the world's billions to peace and prosperity. Also, ancient rivalries with racial and ethnic overtones add grave dimensions to the problems of world governance.

Often overlooked are the religious dimensions of the present struggles that dominate the news. For almost forty years, the struggles of the Israelis and their Arab neighbors have dominated the headlines. In recent years, the Middle East conflict has added further religious dimensions to the struggles in Lebanon and Israel. Armed troops—Jews, Christians, and Sunni, Shiite, and Druse Moslems—have fought for domination in the ancient Bible lands. In Northern Ireland, the struggle is between the Protestant and Catholic inhabitants of the ancient province of Ulster. Both sides commit abominable atrocities in the defense of the faith. India has been the scene of religious wars since 1945 between Hindu and Moslem populations in the northern provinces and in neighboring Pakistan.

The religious zeal of the partisans on all sides of these bitter struggles demonstrate the continuing power of religion in world affairs. As world population has increased, the number of the adherents of the major religions has also shown a corresponding increase. The following table will show the growth of Christianity in the world since estimates have been available.

These figures indicate that the greatest growth of Christianity occurred during the nineteenth and twentieth centuries. Contributing to this growth was the colonial systems of the Western nations. The French, British, German, Belgian, Italian, and American colonial empires became vehicles for the spread of the gospel to subject populations under their control. By the end of the nineteenth century, there were those who optimistically predicted that the next 100 years would constitute the "Christian Century." The magazine of that name (which observed its 100th year in 1984) was dedicated to the proposition that the kingdom of Christ would dominate the world by the year 2000.

Although the church has not accomplished this worthy goal, it has done far better than most people realize. In 1982, a monumental book was published by Oxford University Press

Table 2

Christianity and World Population
(in millions)

year (A.D.)	population	Christians	% of Christians
33	169.7	0.0	0.0
100	181.5	1.0	0.6
500	193.4	43.4	22.4
1000	269.2	50.4	18.7
1500	425.3	81.0	19.0
1800	902.6	208.2	23.1
1900	1619.9	558.1	34.4
1980	4373.9	1432.7	32.8
1985	4781.1	1548.6	32.4
2000	6259.6	2019.9	32.3

entitled *The World Christian Encyclopedia.* Written by an Anglican missionary to Kenya, David Barrett, this work contained the results of the most thorough census of world religion in history. *Time* magazine reported that Barrett had "counted every soul on earth." In general, the story of the growth of Christianity is remarkable.[1]

Christianity in the World in 1980

Out of a world population of 4,374,000,000, about one third, 32.8 percent or 1,433,000,000, are Christians.

The United States. The U.S. had 161,000,000 Christians in 1980. The 7.1 million U.S. Jews are the largest group in any single nation in the world. With its 2,050 separate denominations, the U.S. has the most diversified religious community in the world. In the century from 1900 to 2000, classical

Protestantism shrank from two-thirds to less than one-third of the population. Practically all the religions of the world are now represented in the United States.

Europe. Whereas in 1900 two-thirds of all Christians lived in Europe and Russia, by 2000 three-fifths will live in Africa, Asia, and Latin America. Western Christians (mostly white Americans and Europeans) cease to be practicing Christians at a rate of 7,600 per day. In 1980, the number of non-white Christians surpassed the number of whites for the first time in history. Anglican England and Catholic France have for all practical purposes ceased to be Christian societies and are now being classed as mission fields ripe for evangelization.

Africa. On the continent of Africa, 4,000 persons per day become Christian through conversion, while 12,000 are added to the churches every day through the birth rate. Thus the daily total of new African Christians is 16,000. Islam is strongest in north Africa while Christianity is burgeoning in sub-Saharan Africa.

Asia. The greatest Christian revival in the world today is in South Korea where churches are growing at a rate of 6.6 percent per year. Two-thirds of this growth is by conversion, not the birth rate. If present trends continue, the population of Korea will be 42 percent Christian by the end of the century.

Rapid growth is also being seen in the Philippines and Indonesia. In Red China, which had only 3 million Christians when the Communists took over in 1949, Christians have grown ten-fold to about 30 million in 1980. This growth is the more unusual since it came after thirty years of determined persecution on the part of the Communist authorities. Although most of these Christians meet privately in house churches, the government has recently allowed public worship in churches and has even gone so far as to pay reparations for church buildings that were confiscated during the cultural revolution.

Russia. Though 137 million Russians are irreligious or outright atheists, a surprising 97 million continue to be faithful Christians despite sixty-seven years of government persecution and atheistic propaganda directed against believers.

The Middle East. In most Moslem countries the penalty for conversion to Christianity is death. In spite of this, thousands of Arabs have been converted to Christ. In Saudi Arabia, for instance, thousands of young people have converted secretly to Christianity through listening to preachers on short-wave radio.

The religious policies of Israel are almost as severe as those in the Islamic countries. Even though the constitution of Israel guarantees religious freedom, it is illegal for Christians to proselytize the Jewish population. It is also illegal for new churches to be formed although all those in existence before 1948 may continue to function. Despite these measures, many thousands of Christians live in Israel today. Most new Jewish converts now organize themselves into "Messianic" synagogues and worship Christ while maintaining their Jewish identity.

The Bible. Out of 8,990 ethnic or linguistic groups in the world, 6,850 have been reached through the translation of, or at least portions of, the scriptures.

The Radio Church. Approximately 990 million persons hear the gospel by radio every month. Many of these broadcasts are on short-wave radio which are beamed in hundreds of languages to people in the remotest parts of the earth. Despite the attempts of Communist governments to jam these broadcasts, millions of people in these countries hear the good news of Jesus each week.

Evangelicals. Evangelicals (those Christians who insist on a "born-again" conversion experience) now make up an absolute majority of Protestants in the world with 157 million members. Evangelicals also form a majority of American Protestants, numbering some 57 million in 1980. Large numbers of Roman Catholics are now classified as evangelicals in experience while remaining faithful to their church.

Roman Catholics. There are now more than two Roman Catholics for every one Protestant in the world, according to Barrett. In 1980, there were 809 million Catholics while Protestants numbered 345 million. Eastern Orthodox Christians numbered some 124 million in 1980.

Atheists. While the number of atheists in the world totalled only 3 million in 1900, their number had swelled to 911 million by 1980. This huge increase was due to the takeover of one-third of the world population by Communist governments since 1917. Though Communist governments are officially "atheist" and make life difficult for believers, millions of "crypto-Christians" nevertheless continue to practice their faith.

Protestants. Protestantism has grown during the twentieth century, from 153 million to 1900 to 345 million in 1980. Yet their percentage of world population has declined from 9.4 percent in 1900 to 7.9 percent in 1980. The largest single Protestant family of churches was the youngest group of all: the Pentecostals, who counted some 51 million worldwide in 1980.

Charismatics. The newest wave of Pentecostalism, the charismatic renewal which began in 1960, had grown to encompass some 11 million followers in the traditional Protestant, Orthodox, and Catholic churches by 1980.

World Christianity

The fastest-growing groups are those that are defined as non-white indigenous churches without ties to Western mission boards. By the year 2000, these churches will number some 154 million persons. Most of these groups are classified as pentecostal-type churches.

According to Barrett, "During the present century, Christianity has become the first truly universal religion in world history, with indigenous outposts in all nations and among many inaccessible tribes." It is by far the largest religion on earth with twice as many followers as Islam, the second largest religion.

The kingdom of Jesus continues to grow and expand with every passing day. Barrett's estimate was that every day there is a net global increase of 64,000 Christians by biological growth alone. Added to this number is the number of conversions to the faith from heathenism. This probably totals some 14,000 per day, according to Peter Wagner, Professor of Church Growth at Fuller Theological Seminary. Added together, these figures indicate that some 78,000 new Christians are added to the church every day of the year. These are net figures, after subtracting those who die each day and those who drop out of the church.[2]

Table 3 (opposite) gives a summary of the world religious scene in 1980. Barrett counted as a member of a group any person who had attended at least a funeral or wedding sponsored by a religious group during the previous twelve months. Hence, these figures will not match those of the various denominational bodies; their methods of counting members vary greatly in any case from church to church. They would also not be accepted by many evangelical Christians, who have much stricter standards of counting members. Also, many groups do not count children in their figures since they count as full communicants only believing adults.

Probably the most unexpected finding in the table is that the Pentecostals now comprise the largest family of Protestants in the world. Furthermore these groups are, by far, the fastest growing churches in the world. This is all the more startling, in that before 1900 there was not even one Pentecostal church in the world.

Table 3

Major Religions 1980[3]

```
world population . . . . . 4,374 million
Christian . . . . . . . . . . . 1,433 million . . . . . 32.8%
Muslim . . . . . . . . . . . .    723 million . . . . . 16.5%
Hindu . . . . . . . . . . . . .  583 million . . . . . 13.3%
Buddhist . . . . . . . . . . .   274 million . . . . .  6.3%
Jewish . . . . . . . . . . . . .   17 million . . . . .    4%
```

Of Christians

```
Roman Catholic . . . . . . . . . 809 million . . . 18.5%
Protestant and Anglican . . . 345 million . . .  7.9%
Eastern Orthodox . . . . . . . . 124 million . . .  2.8%
```

Of Protestants

```
Pentecostals . . . . . . . . . . . . 51,167,000
Anglicans . . . . . . . . . . . . . . 49,804,000
Baptists . . . . . . . . . . . . . . . 47,550,000
Lutherans . . . . . . . . . . . . . 43,360,000
Presbyterians . . . . . . . . . . 40,209,000
Methodists . . . . . . . . . . . . 29,782,000
Charismatics . . . . . . . . . . 11,000,000
```

Of Denominations

```
The world . . . . . . . . 20,000 subgroups
The United States . . . 2,050  subgroups
```

If one adds the 11 million charismatics to the 51 million classical Pentecostals, the total becomes 62 million persons. Even these estimates may be too small in the light of the explosive growth that was taking place while the figures were being gathered. At the end of the *Encyclopedia*, Barrett entered the following statement concerning the movement:

> Pentecostal-Charismatics. A blanket term for all Pentecostals, neo-pentecostals, and Charismatics (qv). Global totals (1980): (a) active regularly involved persons, 62,200,000; (b) all persons professing or claiming to be Pentecostal-charismatics, over 100,000,000 world-wide.[4]

Pentecostals and Charismatics

Other studies have given even more impressive evidence of the growth of pentecostalism in recent years. In 1979, the Gallup Poll organization was commissioned by *Christianity Today* to conduct a study of the religious affiliations and opinions of the American population. For those who followed the growth of pentecostalism, the results were astounding.[5]

The survey was administered to the man on the street, and the results were as scientifically studied and interpreted as any other Gallup study. The survey included scores of other questions about religious attitudes. The section on pentecostalism included the following question: "Do you consider yourself to be a pentecostal or charismatic Christian?" An astonishing 19 percent of all adult Americans over eighteen answered yes. This translates to over 29 million adult Americans. If the figure were extrapolated to include those under 18 the figure would reach 44 million persons. Although only 5 million of the 29 million claimed to have spoken in tongues, the figures are of great significance.

Table 4 (next page) summarizes the findings of the poll:[6]

A far greater number of Americans identify with the pentecostal/charismatic movement than those who practice

Table 4

Pentecostal-Charismatics in America

General Public
19% of the total population are pentecostals/charismatics
4% of the American population speaks in tongues

Roman Catholic
30% of adult population are Roman Catholic
18% of Roman Catholics are charismatics
about 2% of all Roman Catholics have spoken in tongues

Protestants
58% of general population are Protestants
22% of all Protestants are pentecostal/charismatics
5% of all Protestants have spoken in tongues

Baptists
26% of the adult population are Baptists
20% of all Baptists are pentecostal/charismatics
more than 1% of all Baptists speak in tongues

Methodists
9% of the adult population are Methodists
18% of all Methodists are pentecostal/charismatics
less than 2% of Methodists speak in tongues

Lutherans
6% of the adult population are Lutherans
20% of Lutherans are pentecostal/charismatics
roughly 3% of all Lutherans speak in tongues

Presbyterians
5% of the adult population are Presbyterians
16% of Presbyterians are pentecostal/charismatics
less than 1% of Presbyterians speak in tongues

pentecostal distinctives such as speaking in tongues. Though this study showed that the largest group of tongue speakers were from classical Pentecostal churches, even some of those groups reported that from 50 percent to 60 percent of their members had never spoken in tongues.[7]

It thus seems that glossolalia is not the only criterion for those who consider themselves to be pentecostal or charismatic Christians. What seems to be the common bond is an acceptance of the gifts of the Spirit as authentic and legitimate ministries in the church today and an openness to the "signs and wonders" that characterized the early church.

The most prodigious church growth in America is now occurring in just such churches. Often cited as the fastest-growing denomination in the United States is the Assemblies of God. Beginning in 1914 with only 10,000 members, this church could claim 1,788,394 members in the United States and over 10 million members around the world in its seventieth year.[8]

Even more remarkable is the growth of the Church of God in Christ, the largest predominantly black Pentecostal denomination in America. Beginning in 1897 in Mississippi with only a handful of followers, this church had reached a membership in the United States of 450,000 by 1964. A census was next taken in 1983, when the figures stood at 3,709,661 members—an increase of 824 percent in twenty years. Although there are those who would argue that the figures for the Church of God in Christ are "soft" and, therefore, suspect, there is no denying that this is one of the great stories of rapid church growth in the recent history of the United States.[9]

The spectacular growth of pentecostalism is reflected also in the local churches of the movement. For decades, the largest Protestant church in the world was the Jotabeche Methodist Pentecostal Church in Santiago, Chile. Around 1970, when the second largest congregation in the world had 15,000 members, the Jotabeche church had 60,000. Recent growth in

Korea and Brazil have challenged the Chilean church for leadership. In fact, although the Jotabeche church has grown to number over 100,000 members since 1970, it now ranks only second in the world.

The largest congregation today is the Full Gospel Central Church in Seoul, Korea, led by Pastor Paul Yongii Cho. By April, 1984 this church claimed some 370,000 members and was hoping to reach 500,000 by the time Korea celebrates the one-hundredth anniversary of Protestant missions in August 1984. When Elmer Towns interviewed Pastor Cho for an article in *Christian Life* magazine, Pastor Cho insisted that he "write that we are the largest in the world because of the Baptism of the Holy Ghost that empowers our people to win the lost."[10] The Full Gospel Central Church also credits its growth to the 16,000 cell groups that provide evangelism and pastoral care during the week.

The second largest church is the Jotabeche Church in Santiago led by Pastor Javier Vasquez. With seating for 16,000 people, the "Evangelical Cathedral" that houses the congregation is the largest Protestant church building in the world, according to Towns. The latest figure of this church's membership was over 100,000 in 1984. The secret of this church's fantastic growth has been its witness teams that preach on the streets each Sunday, and the unabashed pentecostal enthusiasm in their worship.

The third largest congregation is the Congregação Crista in São Paulo, Brazil. The congregation of 61,000 members has an eldership of 750 lay pastors. Also in Brazil is the eighth largest church, the Maduriera Assembly of God congregation in Rio de Janeiro with 20,000 members.

Thus, four out of the ten largest Protestant congregations in the world are pentecostal churches, including the top three.

Table 5 (next page) lists the the largest congregations.[11]

These facts highlight a major development in Christianity in the last years of the twentieth century:

1) The fastest-growing denominations in the world are

Table 5

Ten Largest Congregations

Church	City	Membership	Auditorium
1. Full Gospel Central	Seoul, Korea	370,000	10,500
2. Jotabeche Methodist Pentecostal	Santiago, Chile	100,000	16,000
3. Congregação Crista	São Paulo, Brazil	61,250	3,000
4. First Baptist	Hammond, Indiana	59,600	5,000
5. Highland Park Baptist	Chattanoga, Tenn.	56,000	7,000
6. Young Nak Presbyterian	Seoul, Korea	52,000	4,800
7. First Baptist	Dallas, Texas	22,000	2,400
8. Maduriera Assembly of God	Rio de Janeiro, Brazil	20,000	3,000
9. Thomas Road Baptist	Lynchburg, Virginia	19,000	4,000
10. First Southern Baptist	Del City, Oklahoma	15,900	3,000

those associated with the pentecostal/charismatic movement.

2) The largest family of Protestants in the world are those known today as the Classical Pentecostals.

3) The three largest Protestant congregations in the world are pentecostal churches.

4) Practically every congregation of all denominations have some members who identify with the charismatic movement.

5) The leading popular preachers in the "electronic church"

are well-known pentecostal/charismatic figures such as Pat Robertson of the Christian Broadcasting Network (CBN) and the "700 Club," Jim Bakker of "Praise the Lord" (PTL), and Paul Crouch of the Trinity Broadcasting Network (TBN). Popular television evangelists include: Oral Roberts, Kenneth Copeland, and Jimmy Swaggart.

Clearly, a religious movement of major importance is in the world among us and is growing daily. Just what in the world does all this mean? What in the world is God doing? How could a movement which is so young produce such a large and powerful following in such a short time? In the following pages, I hope to introduce these Christians and a sketch of their history and beliefs to you. These are the "latter-rain people."

THREE

The Gathering Clouds

IN 1958, HENRY P. VAN DUSEN, then president of Princeton Theological Seminary, stunned the religious world with his prophetic article entitled "The Third Force in Christendom." With amazing insight, he announced that already a major new factor existed in the Christian world alongside traditional Catholicism and Protestantism. Pentecostalism, Van Dusen proclaimed, was destined to change the face of Christianity in the twentieth century.[1]

Little did Van Dusen realize that what is now dubbed classical pentecostalism was shortly to break out in the other two camps. Only two years later, the first Protestant "neo-pentecostal" publicly witnessed to his experience, while less than a decade later the movement had entered the Roman Catholic Church itself. Four years before this, a little-known American Pentecostal evangelist named Tommy Hicks had journeyed, without invitation, from California to Buenos Aires, Argentina. Without advertising or outside financial support, he conducted the greatest single evangelistic crusade in the history of the church. His crowds surpassed the records of all evangelists before him, including Finney, Moody, and Billy Graham. In fifty-two days, from May to July, 1954, Hicks preached to an aggregate attendance of some two million, with over 200,000 persons in attendance in a mammoth football stadium for the final service.[2]

As word spread about the mushroom-like growth of the pentecostal movement in the United States, Brazil, Chile, Scandinavia, Korea, and Africa, the leaders of the Protestant and Catholic worlds began to take notice of the Pentecostal phenomenon. "What meaneth this?" became the question of scholars, pastors, bishops, and laymen alike. By 1964, Charles Sydnor, Jr., on learning that the Church of God (Cleveland, Tenn.) had surpassed the Presbyterians as the third largest denomination in Georgia (in the number of local churches), declared that "it is becoming increasingly evident that the pentecostal movement we are witnessing . . . is an authentic, reformation-revival of historic significance, equal with those other great movements of centuries past."[3]

Clearly a movement of major importance was developing into a major challenge to traditional Christianity. Where did these Pentecostals come from? What did they believe? What were their practices? Were these not the lowly "holy rollers" who were dismissed with pity and scorn only a few years earlier? Who was responsible for bringing this major force into being?

Upon closer investigation, it was learned that these Pentecostals emphasized radical conversion, a holy life of separation from the world after conversion, and the "baptism in the Holy Spirit" evidenced by speaking in tongues. Following this experience, all the gifts of the Spirit would be experienced in the normal life of the church. Divine healing in answer to prayer was especially emphasized as was a sudden second coming of Christ, which could occur at any moment. Also characteristic was joyous worship which struck the first-time visitor as emotional and noisy. This included upraised hands, loud praise, messages in tongues, and interpretations of tongues. Fervent preaching from the Bible offered salvation, healing, and material blessings from the Lord to those who "prayed through" at the altar at the conclusion of the service. The most striking teaching was that the gifts of the Spirit or "charisms" were intended for the twentieth century church as much as for the church of the first century.

Many church leaders soon began a crash course on the history of the gifts of the Spirit in the church. Books such as John Sherrill's *They Speak with Other Tongues* and Morton Kelsey's *Tongue Speaking* provided answers for these seekers. What they found was that the church of the *New Testament* was indeed a charismatic one, according to the reports in the Acts of the Apostles. It was also clear that the early church retained its original gifts and pentecostal power in the long period of struggle and persecution before the triumph of Christianity in the West under Constantine. After gaining acceptance and power, however, the church began to experience less and less of the miraculous power of the primitive church and turned more and more to ritualistic and sacramental expressions of the faith.

The Montanist renewal movement of the period 185-212 A.D. represented an attempt to restore the charisms to the church. Despite some early successes, in which tongues and prophecy were restored among the followers of Montanus, the movement was ultimately condemned by the church. The major cause of this rejection was not the presence of the charisms, but Montanus' claim that the prophetic utterances were equal to the scriptures. Many feel that the church overreacted to Montanism in asserting that the more sensational charisms, though experienced by the apostolic church, were withdrawn after the perfection of the accepted canon of scripture. This opinion was expressed by Augustine and echoed by scholars in the centuries that followed. On the question of tongues as evidence of receiving the Holy Spirit, Augustine said:

> At the Church's beginning the Holy Spirit fell upon the believers, and they spoke with tongues unlearnt, as the Spirit gave them utterance. It was a sign, fitted to the time: all the world's tongues were a fitting signification of the Holy Spirit, because the gospel of God was to have its course through every tongue in all parts of the earth. The sign was given and then passed away. We no longer expect

that those upon whom the hand is laid, that they may receive the Holy Spirit, will speak with tongues. When we laid our hands on these "infants," the Church's new-born members, none of you (I think) looked to see if they would speak with tongues, or seeing that they did not, had the perversity to argue that they had not received the Holy Spirit, for if they had received, they would have spoken in tongues as happened at the first.[4]

As to all the other extraordinary gifts of the Spirit, Augustine's "cessation theory" was widely influential on generations of subsequent theologians:

Why, it is asked, do no miracles occur nowadays, such as occurred in former times? I could reply that they were necessary then, before the world came to believe, in order to win the world's belief.[5]

The overreaction to Montanism, which led to a belief that the charismata ended with the apostolic age continued until modern times. Although the Roman Catholic church left the door open to miracles in the lives of certain saints (a few of whom were said to speak in tongues and produce miracles of healing), the church tended more and more to teach that the miracles of the apostolic age ended with the early church. With the institutionalization of the church, the less spectacular charisms of government, administration, and teaching came to the fore as the most acceptable gifts available to the hierarchy.

The view that the charismata had ceased was given classic expression by John Chrysostom in the fourth century in his homilies on 1 Corinthians 12. Confessing his ignorance on the subject, he wrote:

This whole place is very obscure: but the obscurity is produced by our ignorance of the facts referred to and their cessation, being such as then used to occur but now no longer take place. And why do they not happen now? Why look now, the cause too of the obscurity hath produced us again another question: namely, why did they then happen, and now do so no more? . . . Well, what did happen then? Whoever was baptized he straightaway spoke with tongues and not with tongues only, but many also prophesied, and some performed many wonderful works . . . but more abundant than all was the gift of tongues among them.[6]

The cessation of the charismata became part of the classical theology of the church. Augustine and Chrysostom were quoted by countless theologians and commentators in the centuries that followed.

Gifts such as glossolalia (speaking in tongues) became so rare that the church forgot their proper function in the Christian community. As the centuries rolled by, speaking in a language not learned by the speaker was seen as evidence of possession by an evil spirit rather than the Holy Spirit. In fact, by 1000 A.D. the *Rituale Romanum* (Roman Ritual) defined glossolalia as *prima facie* evidence of demon possession. It might have been expected that the Reformers such as Luther and Calvin would have restored the charismata to the church as the common heritage of all believers. Yet, this was not to be.

One of the charges levelled against the Reformers by the Catholic authorities was that Protestantism lacked authenticating miracles confirming their beginnings. To Catholic theologians, charismata were seen as divine approval at the beginning of the church. Catholics demanded of Luther and Calvin signs and wonders to attest to their authenticity as true, orthodox Christian churches. Following the lead of Augustine and Chrysostom, Luther responded with the following view about the signs, wonders, and gifts of the Holy Spirit:

The Holy Spirit is sent forth in two ways. In the primitive church he was sent forth in a manifest and visible form.

Thus He descended upon Christ at the Jordan in the form of a dove (Mt. 3:16), and upon the the apostles and other believers in the form of fire (Acts 2:3). This was the first sending forth of the Holy Spirit; it was necessary in the primitive church, which had to be established with visible signs on account of the unbelievers, as Paul testifies. I Cor. 14:22: 'Tongues are for a sign, not for believers but for unbelievers.' But later on, when the church had been gathered and confirmed by these signs, it was not necessary for this visible sending forth of the Holy Spirit to continue.[7]

Through the centuries, then, Christendom, in its Roman Catholic and Protestant branches, adopted the view that the spectacular supernatural gifts of the Spirit had ended with the early church and that, with the completion of the inspired canon of scripture, they would never be needed again. The Catholic mystical tradition continued to allow for a few saints possessed of "heroic holiness" to exercise some of the gifts, but such holiness was reserved, in the minds of most, for the clergy and religious (bishops, priests, monks, and nuns), not for the masses of ordinary Christians.

This view was the conventional wisdom of the church until the nineteenth century. Then historical and theological developments caused the beginning of a dramatic change of view in various quarters, notably in England and the United States.

As Ernest R. Sandeen has pointed out, the event that caused Christians to take a new look at prophecy and the gifts of the Spirit was the French Revolution.[8] As the revolution advanced, the radicals imposed a "reign of terror" that reminded many persons of the scenes of tribulation in Revelation. The convulsions taking place in France seemed signs that the end of the age was near. Once confusing passages began to have striking contemporary relevance.

In Daniel 7, the prophet had spoken of four animals coming

up from the sea: i.e., a lion, a bear, a leopard, and a fierce beast with ten horns. A "little horn" on the last grew up among the ten and rooted out three of them. This "little horn" was a ruler who would "wear out the saints of the Most High, and think to change times and laws; and they shall be given unto his hand until a time and times and the dividing of time." A similar beast was also described in Revelation 13 whose time would last for forty-two months. As the French Revolution unfolded, biblical scholars were certain that these passages were literally being fulfilled. The introduction of a new "revolutionary" calendar and the installation of a prostitute in Notre Dame Cathedral as a newly crowned "Goddess of Reason" seemed to underscore the apocalyptic event of 1798 when French troops under General Berthier marched on Rome, set up a new republic, and sent the pope into exile. This was seen as the "deadly wound" marking the end of papal hegemony in the world.

In London, Edward King, a student of biblical prophecy declared:

Is not *papal power,* at Rome, which was once so terrible, and so domineering at an end?

But let us pause a little, was not *their* end, in other parts of the Holy Prophecies, foretold to be, *at the end of 1260 years?* —and was it not foretold by Daniel, to be at the *end* of *a time, times, and half a time?* which computation amounts to the same period. And now let us see;—hear—and understand, *This is the year 1798* ;—and just 1260 years ago, in the very beginning of the year 538, *Belesarius* put an end to the Empire and Dominion of the Goths at Rome.[9]

To Protestant scholars this interpretation meant they were living in the very last days. The second coming of Christ was near: the millennium was shortly to begin; the Holy Spirit would soon be poured out upon all flesh as a further sign that the end was near. The long night of waiting was almost over. At any time the charismata would again be manifested in the earth as on the day of Pentecost.

The effect of these heady discoveries was the revival of millenarianism in Britain, a new interest in the return of the Jews to Palestine, a renewed interest in the imminent, second coming of Christ. Also, there ensued a profound emphasis on the study of biblical prophecy in order to discern "the signs of the times."

Leaders in this new wave of prophetic interest were such British theologians as Lewis Way, John Nelson Darby (founder of the Plymouth Brethren), and Edward Irving. In America, the movement found its greatest champions in the Lutheran scholar J.A. Seiss and in the "Princeton Theology" of Charles Hodge and Benjamin Warfield, both Presbyterians. The search for a renewed outpouring of the charismata was far more pronounced in England than in America. In time, the Princeton "fundamentalists" moved to positions defending the literal inerrancy of scripture and the any-moment second coming of Christ to "rapture the Bride," while their English counterparts continued to concentrate on searching for a renewal of the charismata in the church.

By 1830, some preachers began to investigate any reports of miracles that occurred anywhere in the British Isles. When there was a report that miraculous healings and glossolalia had occurred in Scotland among a small band of believers, ministers and theologians hurried to the small Scottish town of Port-Glasgow. After some time, they concluded that, although the gifts seemed real, the happenings among this small group of semi-literate Scots did not represent the expected pentecost. Nevertheless, the feeling of expectancy persisted.

Edward Irving, pastor of the fashionable Presbyterian church on Regents Square in London and one of the most popular preachers of his day, began about 1830 to preach often on the renewal of the apostolic gifts—especially the gifts of healing and speaking in tongues. In October 1831 the looked-for restoration began, as tongues broke out in Irving's church, causing a minor sensation in the city. But London was not at all prepared to accept this phenomenon as the anticipated pentecostal renewal. The following eyewitness account shows the negative reaction to the sensational utterance which interrupted the Sunday morning service:

> I went to the church . . . and was, as usual, much gratified and comforted by Mr. Irving's lectures and prayers; but I was very unexpectedly interrupted by the well-known voice of one of the sisters, who, finding she was unable to restrain herself, and respecting the regulation of the church, rushed into the vestry, and gave vent to utterance; whilst another, as I understood, from the same impulse, ran down the side aisle, and out of the church, through the principal door. The sudden, doleful, and unintelligible sounds, being heard by all the congregation, produced the utmost confusion; the act of standing up, the exertion to hear, see, and understand, by each and every one of perhaps 1,500 or 2,000 persons, created a noise which may easily be conceived. Mr. Irving begged for attention, and when order was restored, he explained the occurrence, which he said was not new, except in the congregation, where he had been for some time considering the propriety of introducing it; but though satisfied of the correctness of such a measure, he was afraid of dispersing the flock; nevertheless, as it was now brought forward by God's will, he felt it his duty to submit.[10]

The woman who spoke in tongues was Mary Campbell. Irving looked on her as a "prophetess." Others felt differently. Thomas Carlyle in his *Reminiscences* spoke caustically of Irving's "dim and weakly flock" and decried the "turmoil" over tongues. He even suggested that a bucket of water should be dumped on the "hysterical madwoman" who spoke in tongues.[11] Yet, to Irving, she was a holy woman who would make his Presbyterian church an even greater congregation than the church in Corinth.

Although the manifestations of tongues continued for some months in the church on Regents Square, Irving never received the gift of tongues himself, much to his sorrow. In time, the Presbytery of London preferred charges against Irving, tried, and convicted him of heresy concerning some of his teachings on the person of Christ. Many felt that the charges were trumped-up and the trial unfair. At any rate, Irving left the Presbyterian church and organized a new group which he named the Catholic Apostolic church. This group not only taught that all the charismata had been restored, but also that the apostolic office had been restored for the end-times.[12]

Even though Irving founded the church, he was not accorded the rank of apostle. In fact he was repudiated by the church and died three years later in Scotland in disgrace. The apostles of the church decided that their order was unique and that there would be no successors. A large body of prophecies were preserved as well as a monumental collection of liturgies that were used in the services. When the last apostle died in 1900, there were no apostles chosen to succeed them. As a result, the church practically disappeared during the twentieth century.

The unpleasantness of the Irvingite experience did not dampen the enthusiasm or expectancy for a new Pentecost among other devotees of the new prophetic movement. British evangelicals continued to preach and write about the expected charismatic outpouring which they believed could begin at any time. A typical treatment of the subject was given by the great London Baptist preacher Charles H. Spurgeon in an 1857 sermon entitled "The Power of the Holy Spirit":

Another great work of the Holy Spirit, which is not accomplished is *the bringing on of the latter-day glory*. In a few more years—I know not when, I know not how—the Holy Spirit will be poured out in far different style from the present. There are diversities of operations; and during the last few years it has been the case that the diversified operations have consisted of very little pouring out of the Spirit. Ministers have gone on in dull routine, continually preaching—preaching—preaching, and little good has been done. I do hope that a fresh era has dawned upon us, and that there is a better pouring out of the Spirit even now. For the hour is coming, and it may be even now, when the Holy Ghost will be poured out again in such a wonderful manner, that many will run to and fro and knowledge shall be increased—the knowledge of the Lord shall cover the earth as the waters cover the surface of the great deep; when His kingdom shall come, and His will shall be done on earth as it is in heaven. . . . my eyes flash with the thought that very likely I shall live to see the out-pouring of the Spirit; when "the sons and the daughters of God shall prophesy, and the young men shall see visions, and the old men shall dream dreams."[13]

A year before, a British Methodist preacher, William Arthur, published his influential *The Tongue of Fire*. This book, which has remained in print for over a century, dismissed the traditional view of the cessation and withdrawal of the charismata by saying:

Whatever is necessary to the holiness of the individual, to the spiritual life and ministering gifts of the church, or to the conversion of the world, is as much the heritage of the people of God in the latest days as in the first. . . . We feel satisfied that he who does expect the gift of healing and the gift of tongues, or any other miraculous manifestation of the Holy Spirit . . . has ten times more scriptural ground on which to base his expectation, than have they for their unbelief who do not expect supernatural sanctifying strength for the believer.[14]

Arthur closed this memorable book with the following challenge to all the churches:

. . . and now, adorable Spirit, proceeding from the Father and the Son, descend upon all the churches, renew the pentecost in this our age, and baptize thy people generally — O, baptize them yet again with tongues of fire! Crown this nineteenth century with a revival of 'pure and undefiled religion' greater than that of the last century, greater than that of the first, greater than any demonstrations of the Spirit yet vouchsafed to men.[15]

The language of Pentecost that Arthur popularized became even stronger in America. The Methodists had always strongly emphasized a second blessing after conversion. Wesley called this "entire sanctification." Many others called it the "baptism in the Holy Spirit," using the language of Wesley's colleague John Fletcher. This experience began to receive a new emphasis beginning in the 1840s, but after the Civil War the movement gained national attention. A post-war revival began in 1867 with the first national holiness camp-meeting in Vineland, New Jersey.

This historic meeting was destined to change the face of American religion. Although it called for a return to holiness living, the call was couched in pentecostal terms. Those who came were invited to "realize together a pentecostal baptism of the Holy Ghost . . ." and "to make common supplication for the descent of the Spirit upon ourselves, the church, the nation and the world."[16] This pentecostal terminology was the result of a subtle shift that had been taking place among holiness advocates for several years. For over a century, Methodist teachers had spoken of "sanctification" and "baptism in the Holy Ghost" as two sides of the same coin. Before the Civil War, however, most recipients of the second blessing referred to their experience as their "sanctification." After the war there was a growing tendency to speak of the second work of grace as the "baptism with the Holy Ghost."

In 1839, Asa Mahan, President of Oberlin College, published a book entitled the *Scripture Doctrine of Christian Perfection.* A defense of the Wesleyan theology of entire sanctification, the theology of the second blessing was presented in strongly Christological terms with little or no emphasis on the Holy Spirit.[17] By 1870, Mahan published a revision of the same book under the title *The Baptism of the Holy Ghost* in which a profound shift in terminology and exegesis was immediately apparent. In the first, Mahan saw "the blessing" as an ethical experience of cleansing from inbred sin with references to Ezekiel 36:25, Matthew 5:48, John 17:20-23, and 1 Thessalonians 5:23-24. In the second, his major texts were taken from the book of Acts (2:4, 19:2, etc.) and from such Old Testament passages as Joel 2:28 and Zechariah 13:1. Pentecostal language permeated the book. The second-blessing experiences of the Wesleys, Madam Guyon, Finney, and Mahan himself were described as "Baptism in the Holy Spirit." The effect of this baptism was an "enduement of power from on high" as well as an inner cleansing.[18]

By 1900, the change to pentecostal language had become practically universal in the holiness movement. Thus, in 1897 the *Guide to Holiness* changed its subtitle from "and revival miscellany" to "and Pentecostal Life" in its masthead. This was done, according to the editor, in response to "the signs of the times, which indicate inquiry, research, and ardent pursuit of the gifts and graces, and power of the Holy Spirit." He added further, "the pentecostal idea is pervading Christian thought and aspirations more than ever before."[19]

As Donald Dayton has pointed out, "by the turn of the century *everything* from camp meetings to choirs are described in the *Guide* as 'pentecostal.' Sermons are published under the heading 'Pentecostal pulpit'; women's reports under 'Pentecostal womanhood'; personal experiences are reported as 'Pentecostal testimonies,' and so on."[20] The word *pentecostal* took on the aspects of a code-word synonymous with the holiness movement much as the word *charismatic* has become fashionable today to refer to all pentecostals.

The word *pentecostal* thus became necessary in the title of most holiness books published in the 1890s and the early 1900s. A typical example was Martin Wells Knapp's 1898 *Lightning Bolts from Pentecostal Skies, or the Devices of the Devil Unmasked.*[21] The popularity of the words *pentecostal* and *baptism with the Holy Ghost* soon permeated much of the evangelical world. Melvin Dieter has summarized:

Pentecost as past proof of God's power, pentecost as the present pattern for the renewal of the churches, and pentecost as the portent of fulfillment of all things in the restoration of God's kingdom among men, became the pervading atmosphere of the holiness movement.[22]

In the light of this emphasis, it is not surprising that a "third blessing" movement appeared in the ranks of the holiness movement. By 1895, B.H. Irwin's "Fire-Baptized" Holiness group was actively promoting a separate "baptism with the Holy Ghost and fire" subsequent to the experiences of conversion and sanctification. The rapid growth of this movement after 1895 gave testimony to a hunger on the part of many holiness and evangelical Christians for a more "pentecostal" experience than they had received under classical holiness teaching.

"Third blessingism" was an important portent of things to come in the holiness movement which produced the later pentecostal movement. It is not without significance that the first person to speak in tongues in the twentieth century, Agnes Ozman, was a member of Irwin's Fire-Baptized group. Such wide-spread use of pentecostal terminology had the effect of moving experience-oriented Christians ever closer to modern pentecostalism.

This pentecostal emphasis which developed in the holiness movement after 1867 also found expression in the various offshoots of the movement in England and America. This is best seen in the development of the famous Keswick "Higher Life" conferences in England and the Northfield Conferences in Massachusetts conducted by D.L. Moody.

The Keswick summer conventions were begun in 1875 as a British counterpart of the blossoming American holiness movement. The Keswick conferences were later dominated by Robert Pearsall Smith, an American evangelist whose wife, Hannah Whitall Smith, also became known as a popular speaker and author. Smith carried the pentecostal terminology gaining currency among holiness believers to the point of doctrinal change. This new Keswick emphasis displaced the concept of the second blessing as an "eradication" of the sinful nature to a baptism in the Holy Spirit as an "enduement of power for service." The experience anticipated by the ardent seekers at Keswick was cast not so much in terms of cleansing as in the anointing by the Spirit. Further, the Spirit-filled life was not a "state of perfection" but a "maintained condition."

This approach caused a rift between the Keswick teachers and the more traditional holiness teachers in America:

These teachings—the denial of the eradication of inward sin and the emphasis on pre-millenianism, faith healing, and the gifts of the Spirit—opened a wide breach in the holiness ranks. The conflict spread to America when Dwight L. Moody; R.A. Torrey, first president of Moody Bible Institute, Chicago; Adoniram J.G. Gordon, father of Gordon College, Boston; A.B. Simpson, founder of the Christian and Missionary Alliance; and the evangelist

J. Wilbur Chapman began to propagate in this country the Keswick version of the second blessing."[23]

The outstanding example of the Keswick teaching was seen in the work of R.A. Torrey:

> The baptism with the Holy Spirit is an operation of the Holy Spirit distinct from and subsequent from His regenerating work ... an impartation of power for service. [Such an experience was] not merely for the apostles, not merely for those of the apostolic age, but for "all that are afar off; even as many as the Lord our God shall call" ... it is for every believer in every age of the church's history."[24]

Although Torrey and Smith spread the Keswick understanding of the "baptism with the Holy Ghost" from coast to coast, the most influential proponent of the experience in America was Dwight L. Moody, the most famous evangelist of his day. Even though he already was a powerful preacher, Moody was influenced to seek a deeper experience by two ladies in his Chicago church who prayed constantly for him to be "baptized in the Holy Spirit" for even greater service. At first resistant to any new spiritual experiences, Moody eventually asked the two ladies, both members of the Free Methodist church, to pray for him. In a dramatic prayer meeting in 1871, Moody reported that he was suddenly baptized with the Holy Spirit. During this experience, Moody testified that he "dropped to the floor and lay bathing his soul in the divine" while his room "seemed ablaze with God." [25]

After his baptism in the Spirit, Moody began to conduct annual "higher life" conferences in Northfield, Massachusetts, to which thousands came to receive their "personal pentecost." In later years Moody turned his attention to education, founding the Moody Bible Institute in Chicago in 1889. The "higher life" baptism continued to be taught there even after Moody's death in 1899.

Moody's passing marked an important milestone in the history of the tradition that emphasized a subsequent work of the Holy Spirit after conversion. By this time, the emphasis on a personal pentecostal experience was no longer considered to be a bizarre teaching on the fringes of mainline evangelical Christianity, but was widely accepted in the mainstream of American and British religious life as an attainable experience for modern times.

A parallel trend toward a new emphasis on the Holy Spirit was also seen among Roman Catholics as the century came to a close.[26] The seeds for this emphasis were planted earlier in the century in the work of two German theologians, Johann Adam Moehler and Matthias Scheeben. Moehler's major work was the 1825 *Unity in the Church,* which depicted the church as a charismatic body constituted and enlivened by the Holy Spirit. The later work of Scheeben (during the 1870s and 1880s) laid stress on the unique action of the Holy Spirit in the formation of the Christian life. The effect of Moehler's and Scheeben's work was to bring into focus a "theology of the charismata" which resulted in a "revalorization" of the gifts of the Spirit which had suffered a decline among both Catholics and Protestants during the bitter debates of the reformation.

Even more striking was the story of Elena Guerra. As leader of a group of sisters dedicated to the Christian education of young girls, she became pained at the lack of attention and devotion paid by Catholics to the Holy Spirit. As a child, Elena had been impressed to pray a novena (a nine-day cycle of special prayer) to the Holy Spirit between the feasts of the Ascension and Pentecost, to commemorate the days that the Apostles waited in the upper room for the outpouring of the Spirit. Against the advice of friends, she wrote Pope Leo XIII suggesting that the idea of a special novena to the Holy Spirit become a universal observance of the church.

To the astonishment of her friends, the pope not only read her letter, but in 1897 issued an encyclical letter entitled, *On the Holy Spirit.* In this document, the pope not only called for such a novena, but directed the church to a new appreciation of the Holy Spirit and the gifts of the Spirit. Millions of Catholics, from theologians to the humble faithful turned their attention to the Holy Spirit in a way that had not been seen in the church for centuries.

Thus, as the century came to an end, both Catholic and Protestant leaders were calling for a new Pentecost with a restoration of the signs and wonders that had characterized the early church. In a sense, the entire nineteenth century was like a Pentecost novena—the church waiting in the upper room praying for and expecting an outpouring of the Holy Spirit with a renewal of the gifts of the Spirit for the new century that was about to dawn.

FOUR

The Rain Falls in America

B Y THE END OF THE NINETEENTH CENTURY, the stage had been set for the rise of the modern pentecostal movement. The three great evangelical forces of the century—the holiness movement, the Keswick higher life movement, and the fundamentalist movement—had all planted seeds which practically guaranteed the appearance of charismatic manifestations in the church. Indeed, with thousands of Christians preaching about, praying for, and singing about a renewal of Pentecost, it would have been most surprising if the longed-for outpouring had failed to appear.

A surprising element in the long nineteenth-century development toward pentecostalism was a general lack of concern about the charismatic dimension of the biblical pentecostal experience. The only groups to experience glossolalia during the century were the followers of Edward Irving, the Shakers led by prophetess Anna Lee, and the Mormons led by Joseph Smith and Brigham Young. Although reception of the baptism with the Holy Spirit was greatly emphasized in evangelical circles, few seemed to notice the proximity of speaking in tongues in the major biblical texts describing the experience in the early church.

A typical treatment of the "tongues problem" was that given by R.A. Torrey in his 1895 classic, *Baptism with the Holy Spirit*:

In my early study of the Baptism with the Holy Spirit I noticed that in many instances those who were so baptized "spoke in tongues," and the question often came into my mind, if one is baptized with the Holy Spirit will he not speak with tongues? But I saw no one so speaking and I often wondered, is there any one today who actually is baptized with the Holy Spirit?[1]

Surely this problem must have concerned many of the holiness and higher life teachers who were so boldly proclaiming the pentecostal experience for their day. Perhaps Torrey's solution was typical of how many others handled the problem:

This twelfth chapter of 1st Corinthians cleared me up on that, especially when I found Paul asking of those who had been baptized with the Holy Spirit, "Do all speak with tongues?" (1 Corinthians. 12:30)[2]

In the same year that Torrey wrote, Andrew Murray published the first edition of his famous *The Full Blessing of Pentecost,* another example of the higher life view of the pentecostal experience. To Murray, tongues was not a problem at all, since for him, they were not even considered as part of the baptism in the Holy Ghost. In his chapter dealing with the "evidences and results" of the experience, not a single charismatic manifestation was listed.[3]

A similar treatment of the subject was given by A.B. Simpson in 1896. As "evidences" of the baptism with the Holy Spirit, Simpson offered the following:

1) a fullness of Jesus

2) a life of holiness, righteousness and obedience

3) fullness of joy

4) the fruits of the Spirit

5) knowledge and light

6) our bodies will feel the fullness ("the fullness of the Spirit is the elixir for body, brain, and being. To be filled with His blessed life will make our feet spring, our nerves steady, our brain strong, our circulation regular," etc.)[4]

This quotation shows the climate of the times. By 1901, many persons believed that some *physical* effects would accompany the pentecostal experience. W.B. Godbey, who in his classic *Commentary on Acts* stated that "they were filled with the Holy Ghost and began to speak . . . ," ignored the glossolalia mentioned in the text and stated that "hallelujah earthquakes" would follow the baptism. As a result of such teachings, Hannah Whitall Smith reported that, at the turn of the century, many persons were desperately seeking a "conscious" baptism of the Holy Ghost that would result in "physical thrills."[5]

The "physical thrills" that had traditionally accompanied the second blessing were such frontier-related demonstrations as shouting, "dancing in the spirit," falling out "under the power," or catching the "holy laugh." All these phenomena were well known, especially among the holiness people. As strange as it may seem, occurrences of glossolalia were rare as the century wore to its close, although here and there a few persons experienced tongues in revivals and camp meetings. When tongues occurred, they were often misunderstood and opposed, though some occasionally seemed to grasp their scriptural significance.

A holiness camp meeting in 1881 presaged the controversies that were to come later in the twentieth century:

One day right in the midst of a great sermon, a woman from Carrol County, a holiness professor, sprawled out at full length in the aisle. This was in itself not much to be thought of, for to tumble over now and then was expected. But the unexpected happened in this case. It kept some of the sisters busy to keep her with a measurably decent appearance. Directly she began to compose a jargon of words in rhyme and sing them in a weird tune. She persisted till the service was spoiled and the camp was thrown into a hubbub. Strange to say, the camp was divided thereby. Some said it was a wonderful manifestation of divine power, some said it was a repetition of speaking in unknown tongues as at Pentecost. But every preacher on the grounds without exception declared it to be of the devil. But the camp was so divided in opinion that it had to be handled with the greatest of care.[6]

With many thousands of spiritually minded people seeking a New Testament experience of Spirit-baptism, it is hardly surprising that sooner or later someone, somewhere, would be baptized in the Holy Spirit with the accompanying charismatic evidence of speaking in tongues.

It is against this background of an entire century of expectancy and teaching about the baptism in the Holy Spirit that pentecostalism suddenly appeared in the United States. All the ingredients of modern pentecostalism were already present in the radical wing of the holiness movement by 1900 except one thing—glossolalia. The first *Discipline* of the Pentecostal Holiness church, published in 1901, contained clear statements on justification by faith, sanctification as a second work of grace, instant divine healing, and the imminent pre-millennial second coming of Christ. All that was lacking was the third experience—the baptism in the Holy Spirit with the accompanying evidence of speaking in tongues.[7]

With this pattern of preparation during the nineteenth century in both England and America, it is not surprising that the students in Charles Parham's Bethel Bible School in Topeka, Kansas, concluded that glossolalia was the biblical evidence of the baptism in the Holy Spirit when Parham made his famous weekend study assignment in the winter of 1900. Yet, when Agnes Ozman asked her teacher and fellow students to lay hands upon her and pray for her to be baptized in the Holy Spirit, *expecting* to speak in tongues, she was flying in the face of history and tradition. For a thousand years, the church had seen tongues-speech as evidence of demon possession, and for a thousand years this experience had lain outside the mainstream of Christian tradition. It was now about to re-enter Christian life in a striking and historic manner.

On the first day of the twentieth century, January 1, 1901, Agnes Ozman, an eighteen-year-old Bible student, received her pentecostal experience and spoke in tongues. This "touch felt round the world," given to a young girl, "made the Pentecostal movement of the twentieth century."[8]

About 115 persons were present in a watchnight service. By the light of coal oil lamps, the group sought the Lord for more power in the new century. As Parham later recalled the event:

I laid my hands upon her and prayed. I had scarcely repeated three dozen sentences when a glory fell upon her, a halo seemed to surround her head and face, and she began speaking in the Chinese language and was unable to speak English for three days. When she tried to write in English to tell us of her experience she wrote the Chinese, copies of which we still have in newspapers printed at that time.[9]

No one else received the gift of tongues on that New Year's day. Miss Ozman thought the gift was uniquely hers and was surprised when others began to seek and receive the experience.

By the second evening, Ozman had received the Bohemian language, and in a few days, Parham and most of the other students had received the pentecostal experience. Soon the students began to sing in tongues, and give "messages" in tongues that were explained through the gift of interpretation. Upon reflection, Parham concluded that the holiness and higher life advocates of the second blessing had been missing a key element in their teaching. According to the students and the teacher, speaking in tongues was the first or "initial" evidence of the baptism in the Holy Spirit, while all the other gifts and fruit of the Spirit would be secondary evidences.[10]

For five years Parham and his band of students traveled throughout the southwestern states proclaiming the gospel of the "Apostolic Faith," as he named his movement. During this period of whirlwind activity, Parham won about 25,000 followers to his new church. He was not able to conserve all his converts, however, since he steadfastly refused to countenance any type of ecclesiastical organization whatsoever. Though Parham created minor sensations in such cities as Topeka and Houston, Texas, during these years, he was never able to spark the nation's interest in the new tongues-attested baptism. It remained for one of his students, William J. Seymour, to become the chosen vessel of the new pentecostal revival.

Parham met Seymour in 1905 when he decided to move his Bible school to Houston after a successful revival there. Seymour applied to study in Parham's new school, and was accepted. His acceptance was remarkable for the times, since Seymour was a black man in the deep South. Despite all the segregation, "Jim Crow" laws of the times, Seymour attended classes and learned of the "initial evidence" pentecostal experience. An unknown southern, black, Holiness preacher, Seymour had previously been a Methodist, a preacher in the Church of God (Anderson, Indiana), and a member of the "Evening Light Saints." In Houston, Seymour accepted Parham's doctrine although he did not receive the tongues experience at that time.

After an invitation to preach in a black Holiness church in Los Angeles in 1906, Seymour conducted what became one of the most important revival meetings in the history of the church. The Azusa Street revival of 1906-09, under Seymour's leadership, convinced untold thousands of Christians around the world that the long expected "latter rain" outpouring had indeed begun. What the eloquent and highly educated Scottish Presbyterian Edward Irving had failed to do in 1831, a Southern, black, Holiness preacher from Texas accomplished in 1906.

Through newspaper reports, religious periodical articles, revival services, and the testimony of visitors, reports spread around the world that the long wait was finally over; the charismata had now been restored to the church and the "restoration of all things" had begun. All of these signs and wonders would be proof positive of the imminent coming of Jesus.

The first news reports of the Azusa Street meeting were sensational. Although the secular press played up the ludicrous "circus-like" atmosphere of the revival, the Holiness press was surprisingly favorable. The key person in spreading these reports was Frank Bartleman, a Holiness evangelist who seemed to grasp the historic significance of the services from the very beginning. From him, Holiness people of both the Wesleyan and Keswick persuasions received news of the events in Los Angeles. The following was a typical Bartleman report:

> . . . demons are being cast out, the sick healed, many blessedly saved, restored and baptized with the Holy Spirit and power. Heroes are being developed, the weak made strong in the Lord. Men's hearts are being searched as with a lighted candle. It is a tremendous sifting time, not only of actions, but of inner, secret motives. Nothing can escape the all-searching eye of God. Jesus is being lifted up, the "blood" magnified, and the Holy Spirit is honored once more. There is much "slaying power" manifest. . . . Strong men lie for hours under the mighty power of God, cut down like grass. The revival will be a world-wide one without doubt.[11]

All of those who heard about Azusa Street were forced to make a decision. Is this the great latter-rain outpouring of the

Holy Spirit or is it not? Since some leaders quickly decided that the Los Angeles Pentecost was not the genuine article, opposition soon began in earnest. Eight months after the beginning of the meeting, Phineas Bresee, founder of the Church of the Nazarene in Los Angeles (whose church was nearby), gave the following critique of these new pentecostals:

> Locally it is of small account, being insignificant both in numbers and influence. . . . It has had about as much influence as a pebble thrown into the sea. . . . The speaking in tongues has been a no-thing—a jargon, a senseless mumble—a poor mess.
>
> There are more or less people whose experience is unsatisfactory, who have never been sanctified wholly, or have lost the precious work out of their hearts, who will run after the hope of exceptional or marvelous things, to their own further undoing.[12]

Bresee, so far as is known, never personally investigated the Azusa Street mission, although he sent a delegation of inquirers who returned a negative report after attending one service.

He was typical of thousands of evangelicals who had earnestly contended for a modern Pentecost and whose theological position helped bring the pentecostal revival into being. Until 1919, his church was known as the "Pentecostal Church of the Nazarene." Others in the Holiness tradition were not as charitable as the gentlemanly Bresee. Alma White, founder of the "Pillar of Fire Church" branded the Azusa Street pentecostals as satanic "demon worshippers."[13]

Despite the warnings of Bresee and White, hundreds of other spiritual leaders came to Azusa Street and were convinced that a genuine restoration of pentecostal power and the gifts of the Spirit was underway. Many critics who came to mock were "smitten of the Lord" and came away convinced.

It was not unusual in those days for a well-educated, cynical preacher to appear haughtily in the door of the humble mission "dressed like a peacock with a jeweled cane." Seymour would tell the congregation to pray quietly for the critic. The power of silent, concentrated prayer was awesome. Bartleman reported that such critics would often be seized with such convicting power that "the breath would be taken from them, their minds would wander, their brains reel, things would turn black before their eyes, they could not go on." Soon the preacher would be struck down, and before the night was over, be found on the floor, white suit and all, in desperate repentance crying out for the baptism with the Holy Spirit.[14]

On the other hand, hundreds and even thousands of seekers came from all over the United States and Europe to experience their own "personal Pentecost." The fact that most of these were serious, well-balanced, and often well-educated persons and that they experienced the tongues-attested baptism in the Holy Spirit is the story of the early world-wide success of the pentecostal movement.

The first sweep of pentecostalism was in the American Holiness movement, especially in the Southeastern states. In December 1906, a North Carolina Holiness preacher, G.B. Cashwell, went to Azusa Street. After overcoming his racial prejudice, he received the "baptism," spoke in tongues, and returned home to "spread the fire."

In a month-long meeting in an old tobacco warehouse in Dunn, N.C., in January 1907, hundreds of southern Holiness people received the latter rain. As a result of the Dunn meeting, the Fire-Baptized Holiness Church was swept into the pentecostal movement, as was the Church of God in Cleveland, Tennessee. The head of the Pentecostal Holiness Church left the church he had founded because he could not accept the "initial evidence" theory of Cashwell, though thirteen of his fifteen churches were pentecostalized overnight. Also in North Carolina a new denomination was born when the Free Will Baptists received the pentecostal experience. They renamed their church the Pentecostal Free Will

Baptist Church. Because of its historic importance, some have called the Dunn revival "Azusa Street East."[15]

From Memphis, Tennessee, three leaders in the Church of God in Christ, a black Holiness church, journeyed to Azusa Street where they received the gift of tongues. On their return, the majority of the church followed the lead of their bishop into the ranks of the pentecostals. In North Carolina, another black Holiness denomination, the United Holy Church of America, seems to have been pentecostalized without any discernible struggle.[16]

Throughout the United States and Canada, the pentecostal flame was spread by the pilgrims to Azusa Street. In most cases, these people had been taught for years that the upper room Pentecost could be repeated in modern times. They saw the revival as the culmination of the teachings of Finney, Palmer, Moody, Simpson, and others. They gladly sought for the baptism in the Holy Spirit and in short order were speaking in tongues, singing in tongues, prophesying, praying for the sick, and in general, exercising all the charismatic gifts listed in 1 Corinthians 12 and 14.

All over the nation the Azusa Street revival was repeated: William H. Durham spread the flame to Chicago; while Florence Crawford carried it to Portland, Oregon; Marie Brown to New York City; and Roswell Flower to Indianapolis, Indiana. In Canada, the torch was carried by A.H. Argue and A.G. Ward. The force of the revival was almost irresistible. Most people who attended the early pentecostal services came away convinced that the movement was genuine. Throughout the nation, hundreds of independent congregations grew up overnight, providing the base for the Assemblies of God, a major Pentecostal denomination that was organized in 1914 in Little Rock, Arkansas.[17]

An interesting case study reveals the force of the movement in the first sweep of pentecostalism across the United States. In 1908, the Church of God in Christ divided over the question of tongues as the evidence of the baptism in the Holy

Spirit. A bare majority of the church constituency took over when the showdown came. The anti-pentecostal faction organized the Church of Christ (Holiness), which remained a Wesleyan body teaching sanctification as a second work of grace.

By 1983, the statistics told the story of the two groups. The anti-pentecostal group had 9,018 members in 151 congregations. The Pentecostal denomination had grown to 3,709,000 members in 7,000 congregations in exactly the same period of time. Similar patterns of dramatic growth could be cited for many of the other American pentecostal groups.[18]

The following table gives the comparative growth figures for some of the major American Pentecostal denominations in recent years:

Growth of American Pentecostal Denominations[19]
Church Membership Figures

	1926	1970	1983
Church of God in Christ	30,263	425,500	3,709,861
Assemblies of God	47,950	626,660	1,788,394
Church of God (Cleveland, Tennessee)	23,247	243,532	456,787
Pentecostal Holiness Church	8,096	66,790	108,000

This growth is indeed remarkable, especially in view of the membership declines in the mainline churches in recent years. By 1983, the Assemblies of God were acclaimed as the "fastest growing" denomination in the United States by church growth specialists. As impressive as the movement in America proved to be, the story of growth and development beyond the shores of the U.S. eventually became the most staggering part of the story. Indeed, the Pentecostal movement is, by all odds, the largest and most important world religious movement to have its origins in the United States.

One of the favorite aphorisms of the pentecostal pioneers went like this: "In the early days, the critics said that the pentecostal movement would blow over in a few years—and it did, it blew all over the world."

FIVE

The Rain Falls around the World

Europe

The latter rain also fell in Europe at the same time as in the United States. In general, European pentecostalism began among the same types of people as in the United States. Surprisingly, the movement did not begin in Britain, although British leaders had contributed greatly to the theological climate leading to the beginnings of the movement in the United States. In fact the British first heard the pentecostal message from a Norwegian who had been born in England, Thomas Ball Barratt.

Barratt, the "apostle of Pentecost" to Western Europe, was a sanctified Methodist minister who, at the turn of the century, was serving in Norway as a Methodist pastor. In 1906, he came to the United States on a visit with the aim of raising funds for a city mission in Oslo (then known as Christiana), the capitol city of the nation.

While in New York City, Barratt heard of the Azusa Street revival and instinctively recognized it as the long looked-for latter rain outpouring of the Spirit. Like many others at the time, he thought it would be necessary for him to travel to Los Angeles to receive his baptism. While waiting to leave for

Azusa Street, Barratt decided to pray for the pentecostal experience in New York City. Praying for up to twelve hours a day, the earnest seeker received the baptism in the Holy Spirit on October 7, 1906. He later recounted his experience as follows:

> I was filled with light and such a power that I began to shout as loud as I could in a foreign language. I must have spoken seven or eight languages, to judge from the various sounds and forms of speech used. . . . the most wonderful moment was when I burst into a beautiful baritone solo, using one of the most pure and delightful languages I had ever heard.[1]

In December of 1906, Barratt returned to Oslo and rented a gymnasium seating 2,000 persons for the first recorded pentecostal meeting ever held in Europe. The latter rain fell in mighty torrents in this first effort.

Of these meetings Barratt later wrote:

> Folk from all denominations are rushing to the meetings. A number have received their pentecost and are speaking in tongues. . . . Many are seeking salvation and souls are being gloriously saved. Hundreds are seeking a clean heart, and the fire is falling on the purified sacrifice. People who have attended the meetings are taking the fire with them to the towns round about.[2]

In a short time, Barratt was established as the prophet of European pentecostalism. Visiting him and receiving their own baptism in the Holy Spirit were pastors from Sweden, England, and Germany. These men returned to their homes to spread the flame and founded flourishing pentecostal movements in their own countries.

Lewi Pethrus returned to Stockholm to lead a monumental pentecostal revival in the Baptist church of which he was pastor. Soon the Baptists tried Pethrus for departing from the

Baptist faith and excommunicated him. His congregation then followed him into the pentecostal movement. Today, the famous Filidelfia Church of Stockholm is the largest free church in Europe with more than 7,000 members that meet in a sanctuary which seats 4,000 persons. This one congregation now operates a radio station, a daily newspaper, and sends many missionaries around the world.

Though Barratt's influence in Italy was not as direct as that in northern Europe, pentecostalism soon arrived there through the medium of Italian-American relatives who brought the message to their cousins in the old country. In the few years after 1906, Italy was honeycombed with pentecostal churches. By the middle of the twentieth century, over two-thirds of all the Protestants in Italy were Pentecostals.

Pentecostalism spread more slowly in the German-speaking nations. One reason was the "Berlin Declaration" of 1919 which rejected the claims of a restored Pentecost with the accompanying charismatic manifestations. Growth in France, Spain, and Portugal was slow until after World War II, when great revivals broke out under the ministry of American evangelist T.L. Osborne. Through mass conversions in the European gypsy population, Pentecostalism spread rapidly over the continent in the 1950s. Today, the largest Protestant denominations in France, Spain, and Portugal also are the Pentecostal ones.

Chile

Latin American pentecostalism, like that in North America and Europe, had origins among Methodist perfectionists. The first showers of the latter rain to fall on the South American continent came in the nation of Chile under the leadership of the Methodist missionary, Willis C. Hoover. A licensed physician from Chicago, Hoover had applied to the Methodist mission board for an appointment to Africa, but had accepted the assignment when informed by the board that

Chile presented the only available opening at the time.

After serving several years as a missionary, Hoover became the District Superintendent of Chile with a flock of some 6,000 members. For seven years he superintended the growing churches while praying for a new Pentecost. A holiness revival emphasizing entire sanctification swept the Chilean Methodist churches in 1902 as they had swept North America in the previous decades. Although Hoover favored this revival, it failed to satisfy his longings. He continued to pray for a repetition of the miracles in the book of Acts in Chile.[3]

In 1905, Hoover heard about an unusual revival in India led by Pandita Ramabai, an Anglican Indian teacher active in the holiness movement. In a girl's school in Puna, India, a remarkable revival had broken out among the students who experienced trances, visions, dreams, prophecies, and speaking in other tongues. Hoover was transfixed as he read these reports in the religious press. Shortly thereafter, a member of Hoover's First Methodist Church of Valparaiso experienced a vision of Jesus Christ in a dream, an experience which was to transform the religious landscape of Chile forever.

In the vision, Jesus told the man, who was a humble night watchman, "Go to your pastor and tell him to gather the most spiritual people of the congregation. They are to pray together every day. I intend to baptize them with tongues of fire."[4] The next day, the night watchman hurried to Hoover with his message, whereupon the pastor immediately called a group of sanctified believers into his parsonage for prayer. They all covenanted to pray each day at 5:00 P.M. until something happened.

As a result of these prayers, a historic revival began in Hoover's church in Valparaiso. In a few days, the fire spread to Santiago, the nation's capital where the First and Second Methodist churches experienced the pentecostal flame. One of the first Chilean pentecostal leaders described the first days of Pentecost in Chile:

It was an astonishing scene never before seen in Chile; the brothers were inspired to dance, to have spiritual visions; they spoke in angelic languages, prophesying about this great spiritual revival. The Holy Spirit took them into the streets. The authorities took them to the police stations as arrested prisoners, but they continued to dance in the stations, speaking with other tongues and prophesying to the same authorities. We were persecuted from many directions, and were cast out of the Methodist temples because their pastors would not accept this form of spiritual revival. They treated us like crazy men.[5]

Despite civil and ecclesiastical opposition, the renewal grew rapidly in the Methodist churches. In Hoover's Valparaiso congregation, attendance skyrocketed as the pentecostal fire fell. Sunday school attendance grew from 363 in July to 425 in August, and reached 527 in September. More amazingly, by October 1909, about 1,000 persons were jamming the church for the night services where the gifts of the Spirit were manifested. When the power of God descended upon the people it was not unusual to see hundreds of Spirit-filled believers dancing in the Spirit before the Lord. The more the Spirit moved, the larger the crowds grew. Many miracles of healing and heavenly visions were experienced.

In spite of the fact that Methodism had never seen such explosive growth in Latin America, the church authorities soon took action against the revival. After negative reports had been sent to the Methodist Missionary Society in New York City, Hoover and his followers were accused of being "anti-Methodist, anti-biblical, and irrational." Many said that Satan and and his demonic forces had control of the pentecostals.[6]

These were the major charges when the trial of Hoover and his friends took place in Santiago in September. The climax for the Methodists came on September 12, 1909, when Hoover and thirty-seven of his fellow pentecostals were excommunicated from by Methodist Church. This decision was confirmed at the following meeting of the Annual Conference in Valparaiso which was held in February 1910. Following the separation, the latter-rain people organized a new church which they called *La Iglesia Metodista Pentecostal,* or the Pentecostal Methodist Church.

The Pentecostals then went into the streets to preach the gospel. Hoover instructed every member of the church, from the children to the grandparents to preach in the streets each Sunday. From 1910 to this day, hundreds of thousands of Chilean Pentecostals have preached on the street corners of the nation each Sunday before marching in a parade to Sunday school and church services. Every train or bus station in the nation became a pulpit for the proclamation of the gospel. Thousands of converts were won to the churches by this method.

While the Pentecostals were exercising the gifts of the Spirit in the streets, the Methodists who excommunicated them withdrew from the expressive holiness-type of worship that had characterized them since their beginnings in Chile in the 1880s. No longer were "amens" heard in the churches, while most forms of public witness disappeared. On the other hand, the Pentecostals adopted a slogan which they still use today— *"Chile sera para Cristo"* (Chile will be for Christ).

An interesting footnote to this story is the growth of the two movements involved in the trial of 1909. At that time, the Methodist Episcopal Church numbered 6,000 in Chile. After rejecting the pentecostal revival, the Methodists turned to promoting the "social gospel" and made their appeal to the small Chilean middle class. In the seventy-five years since that fateful date, the Chilean Methodist church has shrunk to only 4,000 members. As Peter Wagner so aptly stated it, "Many Methodists who blamed the devil for what happened in 1909 have since wondered out loud on whose side the devil might really have been."[7]

The story of the pentecostal revival in Chile since 1909 is

one of the most amazing accounts of church growth in modern times. There are now well over 1 million Pentecostals in Chile, over 80 percent of all Protestants. The Pentecostal Methodist Church now claims over 600,000 members while hundreds of thousands belong to other Pentecostal groups. Recent studies indicate that by 1983, over 2 million Chileans (out of a population of 12 million) now consider themselves to be evangelicals.

In time, the first Pentecostal Methodist Church in Santiago became the largest evangelical church, not only in Chile, but around the world. Named after the street on which it was located, it has been known for decades simply as the Jotabeche Church. By 1936, leadership in the movement was totally indigenous, with the bishop, Manuel Umana, also serving as pastor of the Jotabeche congregation. At the death of Umana in 1964, his assistant, Javier Vasquez, became the pastor. This church has had only two pastors since 1909!

Pastor Vasquez oversees this huge flock through a system of house churches known as "annexos," or "classes" reflecting John Wesley's early organization of Methodist "societies." About 100 of these groups exist in Santiago under the supervision of deacons who are directly responsible to the pastor. Some of these classes number in the hundreds and some in the thousands. At least one has a regular attendance of some 3,000 each service.

The cathedral was built entirely by the congregation with free-will offerings and without help from any sources outside of Chile. It seats 16,000 persons. In this mammoth structure there is room for a choir and orchestra of 2,000 persons (the choir has 4,000 members). The new building was built to replace the old one which had a capacity of only 7,000. Of course, all of the 100,000 members cannot attend every service, so a rotating schedule has been arranged so that the 5,000 or so that live within walking distance can attend every service. The others can come only once a month on a rotating basis.[8]

With Pentecostals comprising some 12 percent of the population, Chile is the "most pentecostal" nation in the world. Since their growth rates have exceeded 10 percent per year in recent years, the Pentecostals of Chile have no doubts about the future of their nation. Some objective observers of church growth in Latin America predict that in the twenty-first century, over 50 percent of Chile's population will be pentecostal.[9]

Brazil

The story of pentecostal origins and advance in Brazil is no less dramatic and colorful than that of Chile. In the same year that the Holy Spirit fell in Chile, a remarkable event occurred in the United States which was to be fateful for Latin America's largest nation. In South Bend, Indiana, two Swedish immigrants to the U.S., Daniel Berg and Gunnar Vingren, were in attendance in a small pentecostal prayer meeting with a few Spirit-filled friends. During the service, a prophecy was given in which the two men were directed to journey as missionaries to someplace in the world called Para.

Since no one in the room knew of any such place, the two Swedes later went to the Chicago Public Library and searched through a global atlas looking for the location of Para. After much research, they found that a province in northeastern Brazil bore that name.[10]

Another prophecy told Berg and Vingren to go to New York City and wait for an unknown man to meet them in a certain location in the city. The man, whom they had never met nor seen before, miraculously appeared and gave them the exact amount of money to buy two one-way tickets to Brazil on a tramp steamer. They departed in 1910 and arrived in Belem, Para, without the support of any church or mission board.

At first, they attended a small Baptist church while they learned Portuguese. In a short time, the Holy Spirit began to manifest the gifts of tongues and healing in the services through Berg and Vingren. This was so unusual for the Baptist congregation, that the pastor asked them to meet with their friends in the basement of the church for their pentecostal prayer meetings. Soon, however, everyone was in the basement instead of the sanctuary. After some "serious tension," Berg and Vingren organized the first pentecostal congregation in Brazil, with eighteen members. They called their church the "Assembly of God" (this was four years before the American Assemblies of God were organized).[11]

The growth of the Brazilian Pentecostals has been nothing less than phenomenal, with the Assemblies of God counting over 7 million members by 1983. This is now the largest Protestant denomination in all of Latin America. The original congregation in Belem now numbers over 30,000 members. Practically every community in the nation has a large and thriving pentecostal church. Many other fast-growing Pentecostal groups have started in Brazil since 1910 and have flourished like the Assemblies of God. The total number of Brazilian members the Pentecostals claim now number over 13 million. Barrett credits them with only 7 million. One possible reason for this discrepancy is that many of these are still counted on the rolls of the nation's dominant Roman Catholic church. In 1980, Barrett reported that no less than 11 million Brazilian evangelicals are still listed as Catholics, although they have joined Protestant churches.[12]

Manoel de Mello, an evangelist of the Foursquare Gospel Church, founded his own denomination in 1954 which he called *Brasil Para Cristo*. In only twenty years, de Mello's group grew to encompass 4,000 organized churches and a church community of over 1 million persons. For several years, he has been constructing a "cathedral" in São Paulo which he claims will ultimately seat 25,000 and surpass St. Peter's in Rome as the largest church in Christendom.[13]

In 1973, it was reported that the number of Protestant

clergymen surpassed the number of Roman Catholic priests for the first time in history of Brazil. Most of these are Pentecostals, although there are also significant numbers of Baptists, Presbyterians, and Lutherans. Some of the more traditional "mainline" Protestant groups have had difficulty growing in Brazil in the face of the Pentecostal challenge. In recent years, many of these denominations have experienced a movement called the "renovation" in which they have, for all practical purposes, become Pentecostal churches. In fact, it is not uncommon for Methodist, Baptist, or Presbyterian churches to add the word *pentecostal* to their name in order to attract larger crowds.

Added to the traditional churches of the "renovation" movement is the fast-growing "charismatic" movement in the Roman Catholic church of Brazil. Brazil has the largest Roman Catholic population of any nation in the world, with a 1980 membership reported at 110,930,000. At one and the same time, Brazil has the largest Catholic and Pentecostal population of any nation in the world.

Latin America

A 1969 study showed that over 63 percent of all Protestants in Latin America were Pentecostals. They constituted the largest family of churches in the following nations: Brazil, Argentina, Chile, Peru, Ecuador, Colombia, Panama, El Salvador, Honduras, and Mexico.[14]

Peter Wagner served for several years as a missionary to Ecuador for the Congregational church. What he saw convinced him that the operation of the gifts of the Spirit was the prime reason for the phenomenal growth of the Pentecostal movement around the world. Later, working with the Church Growth program at Fuller Theological Seminary, Wagner introduced the mainline churches to the dynamic of the Holy Spirit in church growth.[15] One of Wagner's more astounding findings was on the growth of Protestantism in Latin America during the twentieth century. The following are his projections for probable growth until the end of the century:

In 1900 there were about 50,000 Protestants in all of Latin America.

In the 1930s growth had passed the 1 million mark.

In the 1940s it passed the 2 million mark.

In the 1950s it passed the 5 million mark.

In the 1960s it passed the 10 million mark.

In the 1970s it passed the 20 million mark.

Some statisticians project a figure of around 100 million by the year 2,000.[16]

The vast majority of these believers are Pentecostals, and it is reasonable to assume that at least 75,000,000 of these Protestant believers will be Pentecostals. If one adds to these classical Pentecostals the millions of people involved in the "renovation" movement in the traditional Protestant churches and the charismatics in the Roman Catholic church, it begins to appear that the "Latter-Rain People" will be one of the major forces on the continent in the years to come. Indeed, some church growth analysts have gone so far as to predict that over 50 percent of the populations of Brazil and Chile will be pentecostal by the opening of the next century.

A recent sign of the times was the the fact that the first pentecostal Christian head of state in history was installed in Guatemala in 1982—Efrain Rios Montt. One and one half years later, Rios Montt's sermonizing soon fell out of favor with the military leaders of the nation who removed him from office with a coup to install a more traditional leader as president.

Although his term was relatively short, Rios' presidency was significant for the present and for the future in Latin America.[17]

Russia

The beginnings of Pentecostalism in Russia were strikingly similar to those in Brazil. In this case, the apostle of Pentecost to Russia and the other Slavic nations was Ivan Efimovich Varonaev, a Cossack born in 1892 in the Ural Mountains of central Russia. Before the Communist Revolution in 1917, he was converted in a Baptist church and became a Baptist preacher. By 1912, he emigrated to the United States because of persecution from the Russian Orthodox church.

Varonaev first settled in California where, in 1914, he was ordained to the Baptist ministry. He then planted Russian Baptist churches in Los Angeles, San Francisco, and Seattle. Because of his dynamic ministry, he became well known among Russian immigrants to America. Moving to New York City, Varonaev accepted the pastorate of a Russian Baptist church in Manhattan before coming into contact with Pentecostals in 1919. In that year, through the urging of his wife and daughter who had already received the baptism in the Holy Spirit, he received the pentecostal experience and spoke with other tongues.[18]

On July 1, 1919, Varonaev founded the first Russian Pentecostal church also located in Manhattan. He did not remain in New York for long, however, although his new church was growing rapidly. His summons to go to mother Russia as a missionary came through a prophetic utterance in a cottage prayer meeting. The message was simple and direct: "Varonaev, Varonaev, journey to Russia." In subsequent prayer, the same message was echoed in his own heart. This was sufficient to send the intrepid Russian preacher back to his homeland as a missionary to spread the pentecostal message in his motherland.[19]

In August 1920, the Varonaev family left New York City to go to Russia. On the way, they spent five months in Bulgaria where Varonaev organized twenty Pentecostal churches. After visiting Constantinople for several months, he arrived in Odessa in the summer of 1922 and began preaching among Baptists.

In a short time, the Baptists forced him out of their churches since they could not agree with his new teachings concerning the baptism in the Holy Spirit. He then organized the first Pentecostal congregation in Russia. In a short time, this church grew to number nearly 1,000 members. Rapid growth followed throughout all of Russia from Varonaev's base in Odessa. In fact, The head of the Baptist Union estimated that within a matter of months the Pentecostals had grown to over 20,000 in the Ukraine alone.

The spread of Pentecostalism under Varonaev's ministry was nothing short of phenomenal. His ministry was not confined to Russia, however, as the dynamic pioneer soon established himself as the "apostle of Pentecost to the Slavs." From 1920 to 1929 he traveled extensively through Russia, Poland, and Bulgaria. During this period of relative religious freedom in Russia, the tireless pentecostal preacher established over 350 congregations in his mother country in addition to founding pentecostal congregations in several other Slavic nations.[20]

During the 1920s, the Pentecostals suffered persecution from two quarters: the Baptists and the Communists. In the end it was the Communists that ended religious freedom for all the Christians in Russia. In 1929, the Communist government promulgated the infamous anti-religious law which decreed the end of all religious printing, public witnessing, and missionary offerings from outside Russia. Since Varonaev had been receiving support from the American Assemblies of God, he was arrested in January 1932 and sentenced to serve six months in a slave labor camp. The charges were that he had engaged in espionage for the "American imperialists."

Varonaev was arrested again in 1936 when he applied for a passport to leave Russia. For seven years, he languished in prison under intense interrogation. His family has reason to believe that he was executed before a firing squad in 1943 in the grim Marinsk Fortress near Leningrad. His wife also spent twenty-four years in prison before being released in 1960.[21]

Somewhere in a common Russian grave lies the remains of Ivan Varonaev, but his work continues with increasing vigor in present day Russia. In recent years the pentecostal movement has spread to every part of the nation. The rapid growth of the movement, despite all efforts at persecution, led the Russian Academy of Sciences to list Pentecostalism as one of the "most virulent species of religious opium" extant in Russia and the world.[22]

There have been many attempts to explain the rapid growth of Pentecostalism in Russia. Since the movement has traditionally attracted the poor, it has been suggested that the Pentecostals are "more proletarian even than the Baptists." The movement has also attracted many Russian young people. According to Walter Kolarz, a certain romantic mystique drew young people to pentecostal services during and after World War II:

> There is something romantic and revolutionary about the Pentecostal Movement in the Soviet Union. In the first place, the movement is banned and it takes some courage to belong to it. Moreover, the Pentecostal meetings take place in circumstances which appeal to young people . . . mountains . . . forests . . . half dark rooms . . . , and all meetings are secret and conspiritorial. What the underground gatherings of illicit political circles did for another generation, the Pentecostal prayer meetings have done for certain young Soviet people in the 1950's.[23]

Although it is impossible to get accurate statistics, it has been estimated that there are at least 600,000 Pentecostals in

Russia today, and the the figure may even be much higher than this. For many years all evangelicals have been listed as "Baptists" by government decree, although a high proportion of them are Pentecostals. In addition to those Pentecostals in the "registered" churches (those reporting their existence to the government), there are untold thousands of "unregistered" Pentecostal Christians who meet in homes or in the forests to escape the eye of government agents. It is altogether possible that by 1980, the largest number of Christians in the Soviet Union, outside the Russian Orthodox Church, belonged to the fast-growing pentecostal movement.

Indeed, the world became aware of the presence of the Russian Pentecostals through wide-spread news coverage of the "Siberian Seven," a group of two families who obtained refuge in the American Embassy in Russia. For five years the Vaschenko and Chmykhalov families lived in cramped quarters in the embassy basement while their struggle became a *cause celebre* throughout the Western world. Finally, in July 1983, the Russians released the families and allowed them to emigrate to Israel and the United States.[24]

The foregoing stories are indicative of the world-wide spread of Pentecostalism after 1906. One could go on about the origins of the movement in many other nations with the same testimonies of miraculous guidance through the gifts of the Spirit, but the point is sufficiently clear. These early pentecostal pioneers were sure that their movement was the long awaited "latter rain" outpouring that signaled the nearing return of Jesus to meet his bride. They felt that this message and experience was for the entire body of Christ, the hope of the church, and the answer to the dreadful apostasy of the age. Their message was positive and vibrant. They were certain that true believers in all the denominations of Christendom would respond with joy to the good news of the restoration of the charismata to the church. But, to their disbelief and dismay, the church was not at all ready to accept their prophetic message.

SIX

The Rain Rejected

WHEN THE LATTER RAIN BEGAN to fall at Azusa Street in April 1906, the worshippers consisted of a small band of believers gathered in the old tumbled-down building for a pentecostal service. Hands were raised as voices murmured praises to the Lord. Beautiful singing in the Spirit filled the room. This new song in tongues was known as the "heavenly choir." Humble men and women spoke in tongues as the Spirit gave utterance. The members of the congregation were poor; mainly blacks with a sprinkling of whites. The leader was unknown to the religious world, a black Holiness preacher born in Louisiana by the name of William J. Seymour.

On January 8, 1974, one thousand well-to-do believers gathered in Washington's National Cathedral for another pentecostal service. Hands were raised as voices murmured praises to the Lord. Beautiful singing in the Spirit filled the vast nave of the cathedral. Hundreds of professional people, theologians, and ministers from many denominations spoke in tongues as the Spirit gave them utterance. The host was Dean Francis M. Sayre of the Cathedral while featured speakers included Dr. Krister Stendahl, Dean of the Harvard School of Divinity, and Josephine Massingberd Ford, Professor of Theology at Notre Dame University.[1]

In May 1975, 10,000 Catholic charismatics gathered in St.

Peter's in Rome for the feast of Pentecost. The same spiritual phenomena occurred there in the presence of Pope Paul VI. On the next day, in the same cathedral, Leon Joseph Cardinal Suenens, Primate of Belgium, gave the homily while the pope celebrated a special service for the charismatic pilgrims gathered in the great nave. Young people gave prophecies from the high altar under the power of the Holy Spirit.

In June 1978, 2,000 Anglican charismatics gathered in ancient Canterbury Cathedral, in Canterbury, England, the ancient seat of the worlwide Anglican communion, to celebrate another pentecostal service. The same phenomena were manifested: tongues, interpretations, prophecies, and prayers for healing. At the close of the service, led by thirty-two bishops of the Anglican communion, the entire assembly rejoiced as they danced before the Lord and shouted the high praises of God.

The foregoing events dramatize the startling advances made by the pentecostal movement since its beginnings in America. Between Azusa Street and St. Peter's, however, is a bittersweet story of the misunderstanding, rejection, criticism, persecution, and even violence that the Pentecostals endured on their way to the cathedrals.

The first Pentecostals, as we have seen, were enthused and overwhelmed by their new-found experience. They were sure that the entire body of Christ would be renewed and blessed by the power of the pentecostal experience. Many of the better-educated pentecostal leaders took quite literally the many predictions made by nineteenth-century teachers concerning a great latter-day outpouring of the Spirit with signs following. They felt that fair-minded and spiritually sensitive persons would recognize the validity of the charismatic manifestations that had now begun to appear around the world.

This simple and naive optimism was soon dissipated, however, by the bitter opposition that soon arose to counter the movement. Most of the new Pentecostals who returned to their Methodist, Baptist, or Presbyterian churches were soon excommunicated by the churches they loved. They had no alternative but to organize new denominations in order to have places of worship in which to enjoy the "new wine" of the Spirit. Rejection and expulsion was the story of the first fifty years.

Especially hurtful to the individual pentecostal believer was the social ostracism that showed itself in many insidious ways. Children were taunted by their classmates as "holy rollers" while their parents were shunned by the community at large. Yet this price of "separation from the world" as they saw it, was one that most of them gladly paid in their efforts to preserve and propagate their faith.

Much bitter criticism was leveled against the movement during the first two generations following 1906. Most of the critics probably spoke sincerely, but generally in ignorance of the true heart of the movement. There were others, however, who were wildly unfair and bitter in their denunciations. Tolerance was almost a forgotten virtue during those years of the Ku Klux Klan, Prohibition, and Depression.

But, as is usual in the history of such things, this unfair criticism was self-defeating and counter-productive. The more the criticism increased, the more the curiosity to see what was really going on also increased. The great mistake made by most of the critics was to judge the entire movement by the worst examples to be found, rather than judging by the solid mainstream of the pentecostal people whose spirituality, morals, and manner of worship were above reproach. It is altogether probable that the most outspoken critics never saw a fair example of the movement and misunderstood the spirituality the Pentecostals were trying to promote.

The anti-pentecostal argument followed a definite pattern during the century which now can be seen more easily than before. It developed along the usual path of persecution, followed by toleration, and then ultimately by acceptance and accommodation. The following is an attempt to classify these levels of criticism from the earliest days to the present.

Criticism by the Press

The first critics of record were the reporters of the nation's press, both secular and religious. Their reporting was mainly anecdotal, was not theologically informed, and was often done in ludicrous and derogatory terms.

Frank Bartleman, an Azusa Street veteran, remarked of the early newspaper coverage of the services, "There was much persecution, especially from the press. They wrote us up shamefully, but this only drew the crowds."[2] Headlines in the *Los Angeles Times* proclaimed "Weird Babble of Tongues, New Sect of Fanatics is Breaking Loose, Wild Scene Last Night on Azusa Street." Despite such journalism, Bartleman reported that the church was "packed out nightly" while the "whole building, upstairs and down" was "cleared and put into use."[3]

Though such reporting was self-defeating and gave much free publicity to the movement, it was the way that countless thousands were introduced to the phenomenon of Pentecostalism. Unfortunately, this was the only version that millions of Americans were ever destined to see.

The religious press also carried similar items and news articles about the movement. Incredible things were repeated by otherwise discreet and well-balanced editors. Once told, such tales made the endless rounds of reprints and plagiarism that was common practice then among some papers.

Criticism by Violence

After reading the mostly inaccurate accounts of pentecostal practices in the press, it is hardly surprising that persecution and even violence soon followed. Violence, of course, is the most extreme form of criticism. Generally, violent attacks were carried out by neighborhood rowdies and toughs who were non-religious, but who were guided by passions and hatred fired by ethnic and religious bias. For several decades, it was not uncommon for preachers to be threatened, beaten, or run out of town; for tents to be burned; or for the tongues-speakers to be splattered with rotten eggs or tomatoes. Attempted murder was not unknown, especially in the South and the Midwest.

Some early Pentecostal preachers were jailed for their testimony, especially for their practice of divine healing. Gangs vandalized churches while others disrupted public worship services, at times with the consent of the authorities. For several years, it was "open season" on the Pentecostals by the lower elements of society. As late as 1947, a sniper fired a rifle at Oral Roberts while he preached under a tent in his hometown of Tulsa, Oklahoma. The bullet narrowly missed the then-unknown evangelist. Roberts' ministry could well have been ended by an assassin's bullet that night in Tulsa.[4]

There is little point in belaboring the fact that many early Pentecostals suffered actual or threatened violence, since such persecutions were not carried out by theologians or churchmen but by unreasoning mobs. It could be asserted, however, that no other religious movement has suffered more violent persecution in twentieth-century America, with the possible exception of the Jehovah's Witnesses. Also, the story of the Pentecostals is not unique, since practically all other religious movements also were subjected to persecution and violence in their beginnings. This would include the Baptists, Methodists, Presbyterians, and Catholics as well as the early Christians themselves.

Holiness and Fundamentalist Criticism

It is a well-known fact that civil wars are the bloodiest, bitterest, and hardest-fought of all wars. The same is usually true of religious warfare. The harshest struggles are fought by the next-of-kin who actually have much more in common than the issues that separate them. This was especially true among the early critics of Pentecostalism. The extremely harsh opposition of the Holiness and fundamentalist churches can best be understood in this light. Since Pentecostalism began as a division in the Holiness movement in America and swept entire Holiness denominations into its orbit, it is not surprising that the criticism of the old-school Holiness churches which rejected Pentecostalism was especially harsh.

The most common charge leveled at the Pentecostals by this group was that tongue-speaking resulted from demon possession. Typical of this genre was Alma White's 1912 *Demons and Tongues* which described pentecostal worship services as "unnatural," "repulsive," and the "climax of demon worship." White characterized Seymour as an "instrument of Satan," while stating that Aimee Semple McPherson spoke "with the muttering of a witch." Despite her scathing attacks, White's husband became a devout tongue-speaking Pentecostal.[5]

One may better understand the opposition of the Holiness churches because they competed with the Pentecostals in the same religious market among the same classes of people. Also, prejudice is usually directed against the greatest perceived threat. Because of the glossolalia issue, the Pentecostal church of the Nazarene dropped the word *pentecostal* from their name in 1919, being known since simply as the Church of the Nazarene. Other groups including the Wesleyan church, the Church of God (Anderson, Indiana), the Salvation Army, and the Free Methodist church have maintained a similar stand since early in the century.

The above-named reasons also largely explain the harsh opposition of the fundamentalists. Many of them repeated the demon possession theories of Alma White and other holiness critics. For example, Louis Bauman wrote in 1941 that "probably the most wide-spread of all satanic phenomena today is the demonic imitation of the apostolic gift of tongues." He further asserted, "The first miracle that Satan ever wrought was to cause the serpent to speak in a tongue. It would appear he is still working his same original miracle."[6]

H.J. Stollee echoed the same theme. He compared Pentecostal worship to pagan rites among Africans and Eskimos, charging, "This movement is subtle because it is satanic. That is the verdict of the Scriptures. It is verified by the trail of schism, immorality and insanity that everywhere has marked its inroads into the church."[7]

The most hurtful blows came from the well-known and highly respected preachers of the evangelical world, many of whom had taken a lead in encouraging prayer for a repetition of Pentecost in the last days. When the early Pentecostals claimed their experiences as the fulfillment of these expectations, they were cruelly rebuffed. H.A. Ironsides, a former Salvation Army officer turned Baptist minister, delivered the most famous anti-pentecostal polemic in his 1912 work entitled, *Holiness, the False and the True.* As a former member of the Salvation Army, Ironsides primarily leveled his criticism at the perfectionism of the Holiness churches. Correctly stating that the pentecostal movement sprang up among the Hoiness people, Ironsides branded the Pentecostals as "the disgusting tongues movement." He stated that "superstition and fanaticism of the grossest character find a 'hotbed' in their midst."[8]

R.A. Torrey, who had done so much to gain a hearing for the baptism in the Holy Spirit in his books and lectures (as a Keswick teacher), called tongues "monkey business" and forbade their use in his meetings. His most famous charge was that the pentecostal movement was "emphatically not of God, and founded by a sodomite." Of course, the most infamous statement ever made against the movement was the assertion of G. Campbell Morgan that pentecostalism was "the last vomit of Satan."[9]

The last word on the subject came from the redoubtable Princeton Fundamentalist theologian Benjamin B. Warfield who, in his *Perfectionism and Counterfeit Miracles* stated that the Lord had not performed a single miracle on earth since the end of the early church. This, the ultimate statement of the cessation theory, was aimed at both Pentecostals and Roman Catholics.[10]

In the light of the foregoing statements, it is hardly

surprising that organized fundamentalism rejected the pentecostal renewal in no uncertain terms. This was done despite the
fact that almost all Pentecostals accepted most fundamentalist
positions. This was especially true of the doctrine of the pre-
millenial second coming of Christ to rapture the church.

The formal rejection of the Pentecostals from the fundamentalist camp came in 1928 when the World Fundamentalist
Association dis-fellowshipped the Pentecostals, calling them
"fanatical and unscriptural." The later denunciations by Carl
McIntire's "American Council of Christian Churches" in
1944 followed a similar line when he called tongues "one of
the great signs of the apostasy."[11]

This feeling persists to this day in such fundamentalist
centers as Jerry Falwell's Liberty Baptist College in Lynch-
burg, Virginia, and Bob Jones University in Greenville, South
Carolina. Falwell has vowed to never knowingly allow a
tongues-speaker in the pulpit of his Thomas Road Baptist
Church or on the campus of his college, while Bob Jones
University allows tongue-speakers twenty-four hours to pack
up and leave campus if they are ever caught praying in tongues.
In a similar vein, Asbury Theological Seminary maintained a
non-admittance policy for Pentecostals for several years.

The Holiness and fundamentalist rejection of the claims of
Pentecostalism were based almost entirely on theological
grounds with scriptures marshalled for their support. Criticism was done in a sincere, if mistaken, effort to "defend the
faith" from false teachers and doctrines that were considered
to be dangerous. They often tended to stray from theology,
however, and to mix lurid tales of immorality and mass
hysteria which they said characterized pentecostal services.

Psychological and Sociological Criticism

In time, Pentecostalism attracted the attention of psycholo-
gists and sociologists who began to interpret the rise of the
pentecostal movement on purely non-theological grounds.

The first ones to study the movement were as negative as the holiness and fundamentalist critics. These critics were often professors at major universities and seminaries who interpreted the movement in the light of whatever intellectual fad happened to be current at the time. Mental instability, madness, poverty, "neurasthenia," repression of the sex drive, ignorance, and lower class behavior were charges common to this school of criticism.

The earliest and most negative of these studies was done by Alexander Mackie whose 1921 book bore the revealing title, *The Gift of Tongues—A Study in Pathological Aspects of Christianity*. To Mackie, those who spoke in tongues were always victims of some disease of the mind or the nervous system. Taking the popular "phrenology" theory (of reading a person's character and intelligence by the shape of his skull), Mackie concluded that "exactly the same type of mind and, for that matter, the same types of skull that are to be met with in tongues people, are to be met with among criminals." He further accused Pentecostals of encouraging and practicing all sorts of "free love" and sexual perversions. The concluding paragraph written by this Presbyterian pastor was an indictment of the entire pentecostal revival: "Christendom has waited long and patiently to see whether this thing—this gift of tongues—is of God. It is of sickness, of poverty, of fatigue, of disease, of crime. It is not of God."[12]

The most influential of these early studies was that of Yale professor George Bernard Cutten who wrote *Speaking With Tongues, Historically and Psychologically Considered,* in 1927. After a long historical section, Cutten concluded that glossolalia was a psychologically induced state of hypnotism associated with mental illness.[13]

Later books that dealt with the psychological aspects of the pentecostal experience were more objective than the foregoing. Among these were: Wayne Oates' *Glossolalia, Tongue Speaking in Biblical, Historical and Psychological Perspective;* Morton Kelsey's *Tongues Speaking: An Experiment in Spiritual*

Experience; and John P. Kildahl's *The Psychology of Speaking in Tongues*. None of these attribute tongues-speech to personality disorders, although they delve into the psychological roots and results of the practice.

It must be noted that the above studies and other later research largely disprove the theories of Cutten and Mackie. Objective studies which compared glossolalics to control groups made up of non-glossolalics have shown that the former are at least as well adjusted as the latter, and in many ways, even better adjusted. Such were the findings of William W. Wood in his 1965 study entitled *Culture and Personality of the Pentecostal Holiness Religion*. Done at Duke University, this study found that rather than contributing to personality disorders, pentecostal religion helped to reorient and balance the personalities of converts whose lives were previously disoriented. Pentecostalism, to Wood's surprise, served as a solution to the problems of socio-cultural disruption and low social status.

Sociological studies such as Liston Pope's 1936 classic, *Millhands and Preachers*, pointed to the lower class status of most early Pentecostals. Other sociological studies looked to economic and social forces to explain the origins and growth of Pentecostalism. Among these could be cited Richard Niebuhr's classic, *The Social Sources of Denominationalism*, and David Moberg's *The Church as a Social Institution*.

The results of these studies, which depicted Pentecostalism as a "poor man's religion," tended to break down after World War II when the Pentecostals moved into the middle class. They were finally discredited and laid to rest after the 1960s when the neo-pentecostal movement made the first breakthroughs among the highly educated and wealthy circles of the traditional churches.

After making an exhaustive study of the literature mentioned above, Kilian McDonnell in his 1976 study *Charismatic Renewal and the Churches* came to the conclusion that despite the fact that the movement attracted its share of unstable persons, "in very general terms one could say that the evidence points to Pentecostals and charismatics falling within the rather extensive expanse of what could be called normality."[14]

The foregoing psychological and sociological works were valuable and interesting contributions to understanding the movement, their approach was non-theological and failed to come to grips with the scriptural claims of the Pentecostals.

Theological and Exegetical Criticism

Dealing with the claims of Pentecostalism on scriptural grounds as legitimate issues that must be faced seriously by Christendom came only with the advent of the neo-pentecostal movement after 1960. This is the most recent trend in the critical study of the movement and, as such, represents a theological "coming of age." These latest critics are generally respected experts in their fields, and have taken an objective approach to the subject.

In the most scholarly works to date, these writers concede many points to the Pentecostals that many earlier authors refused to concede. Of note, they do not reject pentecostal doctrines out of hand, but examine them in accordance with accepted exegetical methodology. Most reject the claims of instant sanctification and the initial evidence theory connecting glossolalia to the baptism in the Holy Spirit. In general, their work is scholarly and fair-minded, although most Pentecostals would not agree with their conclusions.

Foremost among these works are Presbyterian Frederick Dale Brunner's, *A Theology of the Holy Spirit: The Pentecostal Experience and the New Testament Witness* and Anglican James D.G. Dunn's *Baptism in the Holy Spirit: A Reexamination of the New Testament Teaching of the Gifts of the Spirit in Relation to Pentecostalism Today.* Both of these New Testament scholars make elaborate and exhaustive efforts to arrive at their incorrect conclusions, but, nevertheless, they represent serious studies at the highest levels of biblical scholarship.

This situation was a vast improvement over the years before the beginning of the neo-pentecostal movement. Then, most Christians thought of Pentecostals, if they thought of them at all, in terms of economic, cultural, and psychological deprivation. Only the holiness and fundamentalist critics of the movement examined the biblical and theological claims of Pentecostalism, and these they rejected outright. The larger Christian world in the "mainline churches" hardly knew that the movement existed. The question of the cessation or restoration of the charismata was one that few thought of or cared about. If glossolalia had broken out in these churches, any questions about the phenomenon would have been in relation to church order rather than to theological or biblical correctness.

The road from Alma White's *Demons and Tongues* to Brunner is at least as long as the road from Azusa Street to St. Peter's Cathedral. While few mainline theologians would accept the Pentecostals' theory of initial evidence, there was a tendency after 1970 to accept the premise that the gifts of the Spirit were operative in modern times and to reject the old theory of the cessation of the charismata.

SEVEN

The Rain Reconsidered

THE ADVENT OF NEO-PENTECOSTALISM in the traditional churches around 1960 began to shatter almost all the stereotypes, myths, and shibboleths that had plagued the movement for over half a century. Yet, several years before the first Episcopalian spoke in tongues, significant developments had already taken place which indicated a growing tolerance and acceptance of the Pentecostals on the part of mainstream evangelical Christianity.

The historic invitation to join the National Association of Evangelicals extended to several American Pentecostal denominations in 1943 marked a turning point in ecclesiastical history. It has been suggested that the admission of the Pentecostal churches into the N.A.E. was the first time in all the history of the church that a charismatic movement was accepted into the mainstream of Christianity.[1] Thus, Pentecostalism was well on its way towards social and ecclesiastical respectability before the first stirrings of the charismatic movement.

The great change came after World War II when Christianity at large began to make a major re-evaluation of the movement which continues to this day. At least five reasons can be cited for this new interest.

The Growth of the Pentecostal Churches

After the war, the old Depression-era stereotypes began to break down. The general prosperity that followed the war brought many Pentecostals out of the lower socio-economic classes. According to the deprivation theories popular at the time, the Pentecostal churches should have begun a decline in the face of this new prosperity. Yet, the evidence showed that the Pentecostal churches were growing by leaps and bounds. This was especially true of the churches outside the United States. Suddenly, church specialists realized that the largest number of evangelicals in Latin America, Italy, Spain, and Scandinavia were the Pentecostals. As pentecostal growth rates accelerated, the growth rates of the major "mainline" denominations leveled off and eventually began to decline. Hurried re-evaluations of the movement sparked a new and sympathetic interest among traditional churchmen.

The Ascent of the Pentecostals into the Middle Class

A second reason was the obvious ascent of many Pentecostals into the middle class in the United States. In the general prosperity that followed the war, the Pentecostals acquired financial resources which soon showed up in large and often expensive church buildings. The edifices bore impressive and compelling witness to the fact that this form of Christianity could appeal to the "up and coming" as well as the "down and out."

Pentecostals increasingly were seen in places of leadership in industry, business, finance, and education. A number of Pentecostal millionaires were created by the wartime prosperity. They began to show up in places where they had not been seen before. There were even Pentecostals in the professions; for the first time, the nation saw Pentecostal lawyers, medical doctors, and university professors.

The Divine Healing Movement and Oral Roberts

A third reason for this new interest was the immense success and influence of the divine healing crusades sparked by

William Branham, Jack Coe, and Oral Roberts. Beginning about 1948, a nation-wide interest in divine healing swept America and thousands packed the tents of these Pentecostal crusaders.

By the mid 1950s, Oral Roberts, an unknown evangelist from the Pentecostal Holiness Church in Oklahoma, burst upon the consciousness of the nation through his pioneering ministry in the budding television industry. By the early 1960s, millions of Americans were introduced to Pentecostalism in their living rooms by way of Roberts' ministry.[2]

Suddenly, the bishops of the Roman Catholic church became concerned by the widespread appeal of Roberts to Catholics across America. Leaders of the other mainline denominations also became aware of the large sums of money that flowed to the ministry of the Pentecostal evangelist. By 1967, computer studies showed that Roberts' largest source of financial support no longer was the Pentecostals, but his followers in the Methodist churches. Roberts said that the crowds that packed his tent to its 20,000 capacity were composed of people of all "faiths."[3]

In his books *All Things Are Possible,* and his biography of Roberts, Professor David Harrell of the University of Arkansas credits Roberts with being the most important world religious figure of the twentieth century. With his university, inaugurated in 1965, and his "City of Faith" hospital begun in 1980, Roberts was one of the leading symbolic figures in the emerging charismatic movement after 1960. His joining the Methodist Church in 1969 further solidified his identification with the charismatic movement in the mainline denominations.[4]

The Full Gospel Businessmen

A fourth influence was the Full Gospel Businessmen's Fellowship International, begun by Demos Shakarian in 1950. An Armenian Pentecostal businessman who had prospered in the California dairy industry during the 1940s, Shakarian formed his group, with the help of Oral Roberts, to serve as a vanguard to spread the pentecostal experience to those who might never have been interested in attending a Pentecostal church.[5]

This group, which admitted no women or preachers to its regular membership, became the propagator of a new gospel of wealth, health, and glossolalia. Walter Hollenweger, in his monumental work *The Pentecostals,* stated that this organization had made a "decisive contribution towards spreading the pentecostal ideas over the world" despite the "incomprehensible" (to Europeans like himself) teaching that: ". . . the person who is filled with the Holy Spirit will prove more successful in business, make better tractors and automobiles than his competitors, live in a finer house and, if a footballer, score more goals than the person who is not converted or is not baptized with the Spirit."[6] *Nouveau riche* Pentecostal capitalists were creating a prosperous image for tongues-speakers.

Despite its exclusiveness in relation to the clergy, and its American capitalistic approach, the Full Gospel Businessmen have played a major role in winning thousands of people from the traditional churches to the pentecostal experience. As such, this organization has served as an important catalyst in the rise of pentecostalism in the older denominations. Its major technique has been to serve as a platform where newly Spirit-baptized persons—whether businessmen, ministers, or priests—could give their testimonies on the "banquet circuit" to the encouragement of the businessmen leaders.[7]

David du Plessis

The one person, above all the others, who served as a catalyst and spokesman for the new pentecostals was David J. du Plessis, a South African, descendent of exiled French Huguenots who was converted in a South African pentecostal church known as the Apostolic Faith Mission.

According to du Plessis' testimony, the inspiration for the ecumenical work that he was destined to perform came to him in the form of a prophecy given in 1936 by the famous evangelist Smith Wigglesworth. At about 7:00 one morning, Wigglesworth burst into du Plessis' office and:

> ... laying his hands on his shoulders he pushed him against the wall and began to prophesy: "you have been in 'Jerusalem' long enough. .... I will send you to the uttermost parts of the earth. . . . You will bring the message of Pentecost to all churches. ... You will travel more than most evangelists do. . . .God is going to revive the churches in the last days and through them turn the world upside down ... even the Pentecostal movement will become a mere joke compared with the revival which God will bring through the churches."[8]

This vision remained unfulfilled for ten years, until the end of World War II made it possible for du Plessis to travel extensively. In 1947, he took a leading role in convening the first Pentecostal World Conference which met in Zurich, Switzerland. In 1949, he served a short term as General Secretary of the World Conference. His zeal for ecumenism, however, soon lost him his job.[9]

Although stung by the rejection of the Pentecostal leaders, du Plessis was still consumed by Wigglesworth's prophetic vision. In 1951, he felt inspired to make contact with the World Council of Churches, although he had sternly opposed the Council in its formative stages. During a trip to the headquarters of the National Council of Churches in that year, he was astounded by the "warm reception" accorded him. A later meeting with President John McKay of Princeton Theological Seminary convinced du Plessis that the mainline churches were greatly interested in making contact with the Pentecostal churches.

In 1954, du Plessis was seated as a representative of the Pentecostal churches at the second plenary session of the World Council of Churches that met in Evanston, Illinois. This action, and the fact that he attended Vatican II as the only Pentecostal observer, brought upon his head the ire of his denominational officials. He was excommunicated by the Assemblies of God, whose leaders viewed him as a maverick without portfolio.

Du Plessis became the leading figure in spearheading the charismatic movement in the traditional churches. His work as chairman of the Roman Catholic-Pentecostal Dialogue team and as a leading speaker at hundreds of pentecostal/charismatic meetings around the world eventually earned du Plessis the unofficial title of "Mr. Pentecost."[10] In 1974, a group of reporters named du Plessis as one of the eleven "foremost theologians of the twentieth century." Also, for his work in the dialogue and other contributions to the Catholic charismatic movement, he was given, in 1983, the golden "Good Merit" medal by Pope John Paul II for excellent "service to all Christianity." He was the first non-Catholic in history to receive this honor.[11]

Though his work has often been controversial, du Plessis' place is already secure as one of the most important pentecostal figures in history. His influence has been pivotal in shaping the charismatic movement in the historic churches.

The Neo-Pentecostal Movement

For over fifty years, there were untold hundreds of ministers and thousands of lay persons in the traditional churches who received the pentecostal experience and spoke in tongues. During this time these new pentecostals had only two options; keep quiet about their experience, or be expelled from their churches. For example, under the ministry of Aimee Semple McPherson in the 1920s and 1930s, hundreds of Methodist, Baptist, and Presbyterian ministers were baptized in the Spirit and forced to leave their churches. Most of them joined a Pentecostal denomination since they were now unwelcome in their own church. Some suffered actual persecution.

A case in point was the experience of the Mennonite pastor, Gerald Derstine, pastor of the Strawberry Lake Mennonite congregation in Ogema, Minnesota. Late in 1954, a full-scale pentecostal revival broke out in his church with many manifestations of the Holy Spirit. Rather than oppose the movement, Derstine himself sought for and received the baptism in the Holy Spirit and began to speak in tongues.

Soon afterwards, the church experienced many conversions, visions, healings, and prophecies, not only in the sanctuary but also in home prayer meetings. Services often went on into the wee hours of the morning with many young people manifesting the charismatic gifts. In time, the Mennonite church authorities arrived on the scene and put an end to the meetings.

In the subsequent trial by the Mennonite elders, Derstine was given the choice of being removed as pastor of the church, or recanting his pentecostal experience. Officials told him that if he would only admit that there had been some demonic activity in the meetings, he would be exonerated. Derstine refused. He was then "silenced" and removed from his pastorate. He afterwards left the denomination to begin an independent pentecostal ministry in Florida.[12]

The first pastor of record in a mainline denominational church who experienced and promoted the pentecostal experience in his parish and was allowed to remain in his church was Father Richard Winkler of Wheaton, Illinois. In 1956, Winkler was Rector of Wheaton's Trinity Episcopal Church when he came into contact with a Methodist layman who led him into the baptism in the Holy Spirit.

Winkler's church soon began to experience charismatic phenomena such as glossolalia and prayer for divine healing. As a result of the activities at Trinity Church, an Episcopal commission studied the movement in Wheaton. The resulting report recognized that speaking in tongues could be "unquestionably genuine," but warned of "delusion" and "diabolical deception." It concluded by admonishing moderation since "reason is supremely the voice of the Holy Ghost." These warnings given, Winkler was allowed to continue as rector of the church, a privilege not given to any of his predecessors in America.[13]

The next Episcopal clergyman to receive the experience, Dennis Bennett, was not as fortunate as Winkler, but became a national celebrity and a precursor of the neo-pentecostal movement in America. In the late 1950s Father Bennett was rector of the fashionable St. Mark's Episcopal Parish in Van Nuys, California. A graduate of the University of Chicago and the Chicago School of Divinity, he was the epitome of the sophisticated, respectable, slightly worldly clergy of his church. By 1959, his parish had grown to include some 2,600 members and a staff of four ministers, when he heard about the baptism in the Holy Spirit from a fellow Episcopal clergyman.[14]

After seeing some laypersons in his church who exhibited a high degree of commitment and spirituality, Bennett began to seek answers about their pentecostal experiences. After a thorough investigation, he became convinced of the reality of the baptism in the Holy Spirit although he tended to view speaking in tongues as a "red herring" and quite unnecessary. Yet he hungered for a deeper reality in his Christian experience. As he studied the subject, he was surprised to see so many references to the Holy Spirit in the New Testament, the *Book of Common Prayer,* the early church fathers, the theology textbooks, church history books, "and even the hymn books."[15]

Early in 1959, Bennett finally began to seek the "baptism" with the aid of a fellow Episcopal priest and a young couple in the church who had already received the experience. In a home prayer meeting, hands were laid on Father Bennett as his friends prayed over him. His "nine o'clock in the morning" experience could be considered typical of the thousands that have occurred among the clergy in recent years:

I suppose I must have prayed out loud for about twenty minutes—at least it seemed to be a long time—and was just about to give up when a very strange thing happened. My tongue tripped, just as it might when you are trying to recite a tongue twister, and I began to speak in a new language!

Right away I recognized several things: first, it wasn't some kind of psychological trick or compulsion. There was nothing compulsive about it. . . . it was a new language, not some kind of "baby talk." It had grammar and syntax; it had inflection and expression — and it was rather beautiful.[16]

In a short time, several members of St. Mark's parish also received the same experience. In their joy and exhilaration, they began to use such typical pentecostal expressions as "praise the Lord" and "hallelujah" in the church office and parish house. As word spread among the church members about the pastor's strange new experience, some members of the vestry began to accuse him of fanaticism.

In order to quell false rumors and to answer questions circulating in the congregation, Bennett soon felt it was necessary to tell his church about his experience of speaking with other tongues. Thus, on April 3, 1960, he shared his testimony in the three morning services of his church.

The reaction in the early morning service was "open and tender," according to Bennett, but in the second service the "lid blew off." In outrage, Bennett's curate "snatched off his vestments, threw them on the altar, and stalked out of the church crying: 'I can no longer work with this man.'" Then: "After the service concluded, outside on the patio, those who had set themselves to get rid of the movement of the Holy Spirit began to harangue the arriving and departing parishioners. One man stood on a chair shouting, 'Throw out the damn tongue speakers.'"[17]

After some members complained that "we're Episcopalians, not a bunch of wild-eyed hillbillies," the treasurer of the vestry called on Bennett to resign. Rather than cause further disharmony in the congregation, the mild-mannered rector promptly resigned his parish. Thereupon the bishop sent a temporary priest to St. Mark's armed with a firm letter to the parish officers forbidding any further tongues-speaking under church auspices.[18]

The turmoil at St. Mark's caused a sensation in the nation's press as the story was picked up by the major wire services. *Time* magazine reported that "now glossolalia seems to be on its way back in U.S. churches—not only in the uninhibited Pentecostal sects, but even among Episcopalians, who have been called 'God's frozen people.'"[19] *Newsweek* reported that to conservative Episcopalians in St Mark's "there was puzzlement, anger, even a wisp of envy" although some felt that it "was all a kind of shameful voodoo." Yet Bennett and about seventy of his parishioners were willing to pay a high price for their new pentecostal experience—that of being ostracized from their church.[20]

Bennett was then invited to assume the pastorate of St. Luke's Episcopal Church, a small inner-city parish in Seattle, Washington. His friendly new bishop offered to support him, even in his pentecostal practices, since the church was on the verge of closing anyhow. Free now to promote his experiences without any official hindrances, Bennett soon converted his church into a center of neo-pentecostalism for the Northwestern United States. Instead of closing the church, the bishop saw St. Luke's grow to be the largest parish of the denomination in the entire area. Within a short time, Bennett was ministering to some 2,000 persons a week. For over twenty years, an average of twenty persons were baptized in the Spirit each week at the church.[21]

The case of Dennis Bennett was only the most visible part of a process that had been quietly developing for years. In fact, by 1960, practically every denomination already had many "closet pentecostals," who had received the experience but had remained quiet for fear of displeasing church officials. The Van Nuys incident brought the situation out into the open.

Several months after Bennett resigned at St. Mark's, the *Living Church,* an Episcopal journal, carried the following editorial concerning glossolalia in the church:

> Speaking in tongues is no longer a phenomenon of some odd sect across the street. It is in our midst, and it is being practiced by clergy and laity who have stature and good reputation in the church. Its widespread introduction would jar against our esthetic sense and some of our most strongly entrenched preconceptions. But we know that we are members of a church that definitely needs jarring—if God had chosen this time to dynamite what Bishop Sterling of Montana has called "Episcopalian respectabilianism" we know of no more terrifyingly effective explosion.[22]

During the balance of the 1960s, Pentecostalism began to appear at the most unexpected places and among the most unexpected people. An outbreak of glossolalia at Yale University in 1963 was prophetic of what would occur on college campuses nationwide by the end of the decade. The so-called "glossoyalies" were far removed from the "holy roller" stereotypes. Among the twenty Yale students who caused a mild sensation on campus were five Phi Beta Kappas, who also happened to be Episcopalians, Lutherans, Presbyterians, and Methodists. The speaker who led these students into speaking in tongues was not even a Pentecostal preacher, but a Dutch Reformed pastor from Mt. Vernon, New York, Harald Bredeson.

Time magazine carried the following report on the Yale pentecostals: "They do not fall into any mystical seizures or trance; instead, onlookers report, they seem fully in control as they mutter or chant sentences that sometimes sound like Hebrew, sometimes like unkempt Swedish."[23]

Opinion on the Yale campus was mixed concerning the glossolalia phenomenon. The University chaplain, William Sloan Coffin, Jr., stated that this was a "genuine religious experience" which gave the students a natural way to gain "emotional release from the tensions of college life." Others called it a "gentlemanly fad" and "similar to a ouija board."[24]

Later in 1963, a major article appeared in *Christianity Today* concerning a "new penetration" of Pentecostalism which the author, Frank Farrell, characterized as an "outburst of tongues." Episcopalians and Lutherans were "especially affected" although nearly all the major denominations had experienced the phenomenon:

> Some 2,000 Episcopalians are said to be speaking in tongues in Southern California (these Episcopal developments calculated to give fits to Vance Packard's status-seekers); also speaking in tongues are upwards of 600 folk at First Presbyterian Church in Hollywood, world's largest Presbyterian Church; James A. Pike, Episcopal Bishop of California, confronts the practice in the Bay area to the accompaniment of front-page headlines in San Francisco newspapers; a journal relates that in the entire state of Montana only one American Lutheran pastor has not received the experience of speaking in tongues.[25]

These "neo-Pentecostals," as they were soon dubbed, were somewhat different from the older, classical Pentecostals. An early leader, Jean Stone, editor of *Trinity* magazine, reported that the new pentecostals exhibited:

> . . . less emotion in receiving the gift of tongues after which they are spoken at will—their private use more important than public, more oriented to clergy and professional classes, more Bible-centered as against experience, not separatist, more orderly meetings with strict adherence to Pauline directives, less emphasis on tongues.[26]

The response of most church leaders to this "new penetration" was a general mood of caution and forbearance. Few desired to force the new wave of pentecostals from their churches as had been done a half-century before. The one churchman who objected the loudest to these developments was James A. Pike, Episcopal Bishop of California. In May of 1963, this prelate issued a 2,500 word letter to all 125 of his parishes which forbade speaking in tongues in the churches and which described glossolalia as "heresy in embryo." He also stated that "this particular phenomenon has reached a point where it is dangerous to the peace and unity of the church and a threat to sound doctrine and policy." Yet occasionally, while making the rounds of his churches, Pike would be confronted by a congregation and its priest who would break out into spontaneous singing in other tongues.[27]

Joining with Pike in opposition to the movement was the California Methodist bishop, Gerald Kennedy, who dismissed the movement by saying, "in the past there have been movements of this sort, but they never did the church any good."[28]

Despite these warnings, there were thousands of churchmen, both clergy and lay, who felt that the pentecostal revival was the best hope of the church. One Baptist leader went so far as to say that for the world "the choice is Pentecost or holocaust." Throughout the decade the movement continued to grow rapidly with leading pastors of many denominations following Bennett's lead in openly espousing Pentecostalism. Such early leaders as Howard Ervin (American Baptist), Harald Bredesen (Dutch Reformed), Howard Conatser (Southern Baptist), Ross Whetstone (United Methodist), Nelson Litwiler (Mennonite), Warren Black (Nazarene), and Larry Christenson (American Lutheran Church) gave impetus to the movement. In a historic tour of Germany in 1964, Christenson sparked a neo-pentecostal revival which eventually saw much of the German nobility, both Catholic and Protestant, swept into the movement.[29]

By the end of the decade of the 1960s, Pentecostalism, roundly rejected a half-century before by the mainline Protestant churches, began a triumphal reentry into the mainstream of those very churches. The cycle was complete. The movement was returning with a new fire and vigor to find a place of acceptance among its former critics and enemies. The "new wine" of the Spirit was now pouring into the "old bottles" of the traditional churches. The great problem to be faced was whether the wine would burst the old bottles or if it could be successfully contained. Only time could answer that question.

Within a decade of Bennett's experience, estimates were that 10 percent of the clergy and 1,000,000 of the laity in the mainline churches had received the baptism in the Holy Spirit and remained in their churches. Many of the older classical Pentecostals were bewildered by these developments and could not understand why their neo-pentecostal brethren seemed to have escaped the suffering and persecution that had been the lot of the earlier pentecostal pioneers. Yet, there was a general feeling of joy and thanksgiving that others were finally enjoying the reality of the Spirit's fullness.

EIGHT

The Rain Falls
on Catholics

PERHAPS THE GREATEST SURPRISE in the whole pentecostal tradition was the sudden appearance of Catholic pentecostalism in 1967. Though Catholics had shown a greater interest in the Holy Spirit during the nineteenth century, the struggles over the gifts of the Spirit, speaking in tongues, and the doctrine of "initial evidence" had been a Protestant problem with little concern for Catholics. Most Protestants assumed that Catholics were not even Christians, much less candidates for the baptism in the Holy Spirit. On their part, Catholics before Vatican II tended to view Protestants as either heretics or as sub-normal Christians without authentic clergy or valid sacraments.

For most of the century, ecumenical relations were also a Protestant preoccupation. The Federal and World Councils of churches were entirely made up of Protestant and Orthodox Christians with no Catholic participation and seemingly little or no interest. On the Protestant side, the ecumenical movement was entirely an enterprise of the "liberal" churches, although the original ecumenical impulses were generated by evangelicals in the nineteenth century.

One reason for the Catholic church's lack of interest in ecumenism in America was the great growth of the church in the last half of the nineteenth century. In the 1880s millions of Catholic immigrants flooded into America from Southern and Eastern Europe. By 1900, the Roman Catholic church was by far the largest denomination in the United States. The first half of the twentieth century continued to be a period of unbroken growth in both numbers and influence for the American Catholic church. After World War II, and especially after the election of John F. Kennedy to the presidency in 1960, Catholics began to speak of the "post-Protestant era" and of the day when an absolute majority of Americans would belong to the Roman church.

This dream was to be rudely shaken by the end of the 1960s as the Catholic church in America experienced changes so dramatic that one could hardly recognize it as the same church. Between 1960 and 1970, the church ended its long history of consistent growth. Catholic families became smaller as a result of the wide-spread practice of artificial birth control in open disregard for the teachings of the church. The few conversions to the faith came mainly as the result of mixed marriages with non-Catholics.

Then came the disasters that began to stagger the church. Thousands of priests, monks, and nuns began to forsake their vocations and return to the secular world. The system of Roman Catholic parochial schools, once the crowning gem of the American church, began to close their doors until an average of one school per week was being closed. The number of seminarians saw similar declines. Now Protestants and Catholics together began to speak of a "post-Christian America," as similar declines began to appear in most of the mainline Protestant denominations.

At the beginning of the 1960s, Pope John XXIII sent a tremor through the religious world by calling together the first council in nearly a century. The new council, called Vatican II, met from 1962 to 1965. According to Pope John, the council was for the purpose of "opening the windows so that the church could get a breath of fresh air." As they gathered in Rome, the 2,500 bishops from all parts of the world spoke openly of a "new Reformation" within the church—even to the point of the "reformulation of doctrines." This was the first time such language had been used in the church since Martin Luther's day.[1]

Pope John had also spoken of the council prophetically as a "new Pentecost" and directed every Catholic in the world to pray daily during the three year's duration of the conclave: "Lord renew your wonders in this our day as by a new Pentecost." Could he know that this very prayer would be fulfilled within a year of the closing of the Council? In fact, one of the four Presidents of Vatican II, Leon Joseph Cardinal Suenens of Belgium, would play a leading part in the charismatic renewal which shortly broke out in the church.

What has happened in Roman Catholicism since 1962 has been more than a "reformation"—it has been, in the words of David F. Wells, a *Revolution in Rome.* Every concerned Protestant should read this book in order to understand recent events in the Roman church. For the first time since the Council of Trent in the sixteenth century, the Catholic church abandoned its monolithic "fortress theology" designed to halt the progress of the Protestant reformation, and opened the door for many competing theologies to exist and to contend for influence within the church.[2]

The Second Vatican Council ended in 1965 with a revolutionary program that took years to be fully implemented in Catholic churches around the world. The most striking change required the mass to be said in the languages of the people rather than in Latin. The priests also were required to face the congregation during the service. Hymns were sung by the congregations, instead of being chanted only by the priests and choirs. The scriptures were read by the laity as well as by the clergy. Catholics were encouraged to pray with other Christians, although intercommunion was still forbidden. The informal "folk mass" (or guitar mass) was allowed. Nuns were permitted to abandon their traditional habits for conventional dress.

Because of these changes, which indeed appeared too

revolutionary to traditionalists, the church became much less "strange" to Protestants, especially when Catholics began to sing the "theme song of the Reformation," Martin Luther's "A Mighty Fortress Is Our God." For the first time, Catholic priests began to share in Protestant services and Protestants were invited to speak in Catholic services. A new ecumenical age began in 1960 with the establishment of the Secretariat for Christian Unity in Rome, which immediately initiated dialogues with the Protestant churches. The fact that John XXIII spoke of Protestants as "separated brethren" opened the way for a mutual respect and appreciation that made ecumenical dialogue possible.

It was in the aftermath of these amazing changes that the pentecostal movement suddenly appeared in the American church. In some ways the phenomenon of Catholic Pentecostalism was an unexpected and miraculous event, but a closer study shows that there were many developments over a long period of time which prepared the ground for the "latter rain" to fall in the Roman church. In *Aspects of Pentecostal/ Charismatic Origins,* Father Edward O'Connor listed the following "hidden roots" of the charismatic renewal movement in the Catholic church:[3]

Pope Leo XIII and Elena Guerra

In 1897, Pope Leo XIII called for every Catholic in the world to say a novena annually to the Holy Spirit between the feasts of Ascension and Pentecost, at the suggestion of Elena Guerra, as we discussed earlier. (See pp. 41-42.)

The Theology of Charisms

As we also have seen, the nineteenth-century German theologians, Moehler and Scheeben opened a whole new school of interpretation of the ministries of the church. Their emphasis on the importance of the charisms in the church in modern times began to break down the generally accepted view of the cessation of the charismata. Both of these theologians broke new ground in relation to the Holy Spirit that was destined to bear much fruit in Vatican II and in the charismatic movement which followed the Council.

The Liturgical Movement

A development of extreme importance was the liturgical reform effort which drastically changed the forms of Catholic worship. The liturgical movement also had nineteenth-century roots which came to fruition in the twentieth century. Essentially, the movement was concerned with helping Christians understand and participate in the words and forms of public worship in order to make the church more meaningful to modern man. Implicit in the movement was the reform of public worship in both words and texts.

The roots of the movement in the Roman Catholic church lay in the romantic movement of the 1800s and first found success in the monasteries. In general, those promoting the reform wished the church to be seen less as a juridical body and more as a worshipping organism. By the twentieth century, the movement had moved out of the monasteries and into the mainstream of the church.

After World War II, Pope Pius XII gave impetus to the movement in his encyclical on the liturgy entitled, "Mediator Dei," in which he authorized changes in the rites for Holy Week and called for more lay participation in the mass.

Liturgical reform entered the full lifestream of the church, however, with the Second Vatican Council. New texts of the liturgy reflected the great advances in biblical studies made by the church in the previous decades. Also such innovations as the introduction of guitars and hand-clapping, and a more biblically oriented sermon added many of the elements that were instantly adopted by the charismatics after Vatican II.

The liturgical movement among Protestants led to more

frequent celebrations of the Eucharist, a greater appreciation for the traditional "Catholic" roots of Christian worship, and an updating of archaic expressions of worship. On both Protestant and Catholic sides, there was a deeper appreciation of the liturgy as a proclamation of the gospel.

The Lay Movement

One of the bitter controversies of the Reformation concerned the place of laymen in the church. Martin Luther's teaching on the "priesthood of all believers" seemed to Catholics to be an attack on the unique ministry of the priesthood. The resulting positions adopted at the Council of Trent were primarily in reaction to the challenge of the Reformers who seemed to be granting all the privileges of the clergy to unordained laymen. For centuries, the Catholic laity, for all practical purposes, had no part to play in the liturgies or the leadership of the church.

The dignity and authentic ministry of laymen in the Catholic church has come about due to the efforts of many important lay persons who in the past three centuries who became effective spokesmen for the church. Also contributing to the rise of the layman was Pope Pius X (1903-14) who proclaimed that the laymen were not only "crisis ministers" in the absence of priests, but were to:

> . . . share in his priestly function of offering spiritual worship for the glory of God and the salvation of men. For this reason, the laity, dedicated to Christ and anointed by the Holy Spirit, are marvelously called and equipped to produce in themselves ever more abundant fruits of the Holy Spirit.[4]

It is important to note that the first Catholic charismatic leaders were laymen deeply involved in the liturgical reform movement before their baptism in the Holy Spirit in 1967.

It would be impossible to imagine the pentecostal movement in the Catholic church without the large and determinative role played by thousands of talented lay leaders who gave a lay imprint to the movement.

The Biblical Movement

Another major theme of the Protestant Reformation was a tremendous emphasis on scripture as the norm for faith and practice among Christians. Because of an overreaction to this Protestant position, Catholics continued to stress the importance of tradition as well as scripture as a source for authority in the church. The divisions brought on by the Reformation caused a fear among Catholics of Bible reading by the untrained and of the possibility of heresy and schism.

Although Catholics honored and reverenced the Bible as the word of God, they seldom read it simply for devotional purposes. Meanwhile, scholarly study of the scriptures suffered greatly among Catholics. While Protestants engaged in profound biblical research from Luther's day onward, Catholic biblical studies lagged behind. By the nineteenth and twentieth centuries, the greatest biblical research and scholarship in the world was being done by Protestants. For Catholics, the scriptures were read in the mass but not read by the masses.

After World War II, there occurred a resurgence of biblical scholarship among Catholics around the world. A great effort was made on the part of Catholic scholars to catch up with their Protestant brothers in the academic understanding of the word of God.

It was the charismatic renewal, however, that brought to the fore a hunger to read the Bible as a daily spiritual resource for the average church member. An intense taste for reading, enjoying, and applying the scriptures to everyday life was one of the most striking aspects of the renewal after 1967. But the roots of a resurgence in biblical studies had already taken place in the church before that time.

The Ecumenical Movement

Like the biblical movement, the ecumenical movement had its origins in nineteenth-century Protestantism, flowered in the middle of the twentieth century, and only then sent its roots into the Roman Catholic church.

Ecumenism has a long and varied history in the life of the church. The Great Schism of 1054 between the Roman Catholic church and Eastern Orthodoxy has not been healed to this day, despite many attempts at reconciliation. The schisms of the Reformation period also continue after 500 years. The present religious settlement came as a political result of the Peace of Westphalia in 1648, when the European powers accepted pluralism and denominationalism. The "toleration of separation" which became the order of the day in the seventeenth century has persisted till now.

The road from pluralism back to ecumenism began with the creation of the London Sunday School Union in 1803, which marked the first joint effort of separate denominations since the Reformation. Other examples of nineteenth century co-operation included the American Bible Society (1816), the YMCA (1851), and the Christian Endeavor (1881).

Twentieth-century ecumenism began with the Edinburgh Conference of 1910, which sought to coordinate the world missions efforts of several evangelical denominations. The new idea then gaining currency was that competing missions programs gave a poor impression of Christian unity in pagan nations. Other twentieth-century developments included: the World Conference on Faith and Order (1927), the National Association of Evangelicals (1943), and the World Council of Churches (1948).

For Roman Catholics, after the Council of Trent (1545-1563), the road to unity meant only one thing, a return to Rome on the part of the Protestants. In 1928, Pope Pius XI reaffirmed the traditional Catholic position in his encyclical *Mortalium Animos* stating that the only avenue of unity was conversion to the Roman Catholic church and submission to the papacy and the canonical and visible structures of the church. Perhaps because of the twin challenges of Fascism and Communism, coupled with the world Depression, the Catholic view of ecumenism began to change in the late 1930s. The dislocations and persecutions suffered by Catholics, Protestants, and especially the Jews of Europe caused a new openness after World War II that had not been seen in 400 years. The apostle of the most recent view of unity in the church was Yves Congar, a French Dominican, who in 1937 published *Chrétiens Désunis*, the textbook of modern Catholic ecumenism. In this epochal work, Congar pointed out the possibility that some authentic Catholic elements may have been richly developed in some non-Roman communions. Future unity would not obscure these differences in a "lowest common denominator" fashion, but would be a "sharing of treasures" across denominational lines.[5]

The man who began to put Congar's ideas into effect was Augustin Cardinal Bea who was responsible for the creation of the Secretariat for the Promotion of Christian Unity in 1960. This body began to conduct "dialogues" with other Christian bodies after 1960 that continue to this day.

In Vatican II, the vision of Congar became the official position of the Roman Catholic church. By official decree of the council, the church of Jesus Christ "subsists" (rather than "consists") in the Roman Catholic church. Other Christians are "separated brethren." The ecumenical task is, therefore, to discover the authentic elements in churches not in communion with the Roman Catholic church. Other Christian churches are "sister churches" which also "subsist" as part of the universal church, although the liturgies and theologies of these churches might not be as fully and richly developed as in the Roman communion.

If the charismatic renewal had begun in the Roman Catholic church before Vatican II, it would probably have been seen as a "Protestant" phenomenon and therefore forbidden to Catholics. But, by 1967, when glossolalia first appeared publicly in Catholic circles, Pentecostalism was seen as one of the "treasures" of the church to be freely shared by Catholics.

The Cursillo Movement

The Cursillo movement began in Spain in 1949 as an attempt to renew the personal faith of Catholics by means of a three-day retreat called *cursillo* (i.e., "short course"). Originally called the *Cursillo de Cristianidad*, it was first used by Bishop Juan Hervas of Ciudad Real, Spain. The movement spread to Latin America in the 1950s and eventually to the United States by way of the Hispanics of the Southwest.

Cursillo consists of five "meditations" and five lessons on Christian doctrine given by priests and lay persons to church members who wish to deepen their faith. Discussion sessions show how to make practical applications of the ten talks. With the number of participants usually about forty persons, the sessions are enlivened with a spirit of conviviality including songs and skits.

The effect of the cursillo was to evangelize Catholics who had been "sacramentalized" but who lacked a deep understanding of what it meant to be a Christian. Many of the first pentecostal Catholics not only had attended cursillos, but were leaders in the movement.

Vatican II, Pope John XXIII, and Cardinal Suenens

Pope John XXIII convened Vatican II in 1962 while many of these reform movements were reaching their peak of influence. Never was a council more timely to catch the "winds of the Spirit" that were blowing in the church. As Catholics followed Pope John in praying for a renewal of signs and wonders "in this our day as by a new Pentecost," steps were taken in the council to assure that such a Pentecost would be accepted when it did occur.

Pope John had called the council as a "sudden inspiration"

of the Holy Spirit directed towards advancing Christian unity. In the last message he gave to the bishops, John predicted that when all the reforms and decrees of the Council had been put into effect, "then will dawn the new Pentecost which is the object of our yearning."[6]

One of the four "presidents" of the council was the Primate of Belgium, Leon Joseph Cardinal Suenens, who was known as one of the "liberal" prelates calling for change and renewal in the church. The only classical Pentecostal leader present was David du Plessis who came as an official "observer." Both Suenens and du Plessis were destined to play major roles in the Catholic charismatic renewal that unfolded shortly after the completion of the Council.

As Vatican II progressed, many documents reflected an emphasis on the Holy Spirit and the charismatic nature of the church. Leading in the movement to stress the person and work of the Holy Spirit were the bishops from Chile. This nation, as we have seen, had experienced a mighty pentecostal movement since 1909, and this may have influenced the Chilean prelates. Altogether the Holy Spirit was mentioned 258 times in the conciliar documents.

When the old question of the cessation of the charismata surfaced, the council came down squarely on the side of the present-day manifestation of all the gifts of the Spirit. The issue was joined after the first reading of the Constitution on the Church which stated that the Lord allotted his gifts "to everyone according as He will (I Cor. 12:11), and he distributes special graces among the faithful of every rank." It further stated that these charismatic gifts were "widely diffused" and are "to be received with thanksgiving and consolation for they are exceedingly suitable and useful for the needs of the church."

During the discussions that followed this reading, Cardinal Ruffini of Palermo, Italy, offered the following protest:

It plainly implies that in our age many of the faithful are endowed with many charismatic gifts, but this is plainly contradicted by history and by daily experience. For the charisms . . . were abundant at the beginning of the church; but after that they gradually decreased and have almost completely ceased. . . . Contrary to the opinion of many of our separated brethren, who speak freely of the ministry of charismatics in the church, they are extremely rare and quite exceptional.[7]

Many of the bishops immediately disagreed with this statement of the traditional views of the church. On behalf of these bishops, Cardinal Suenens gave the classic reply which later became a "Magna Carta" for the charismatics in the church:

This document says very little about the charisms of the faithful; this can suggest the impression that we are dealing here with a phenomenon that is merely peripheral and accidental to the life of the Church. But it is now time to bring out more explicitly and thoroughly the vital importance of these charisms for the building up of the Mystical Body. We must at all costs avoid giving the impression that the hierarchical structure of the Church is an administrative apparatus with no intimate connection with the charismatic gifts of the Holy Spirit which are diffused throughout the Church.

To St. Paul, the Church of Christ does not appear as some administrative organization, but as a living, organic ensemble of gifts, charisms and services. The Holy Spirit is given to all Christians, and to each one in particular; and He in turn gives to each and every one gifts and charisms "which differ according to the grace bestowed upon us" (Rom. 12:6).[8]

Suenens's plea won out over the traditionalist view and the groundwork was laid for the approval of the charismatic renewal only three years later. Usually the Spirit moves "wherever he wills," and the theologians attempt to explain things after the fact. This time, the theologians explained and approved charismatic renewal before it began. This is one of those unique times in history when the theologians were ahead of the prophets.

A Surprise of the Holy Spirit

With all of this preparation, it was nearly inevitable that Pentecostalism would break out in the Roman Catholic church. The only question was where it would happen, and when it would begin. These questions were soon answered in what Cardinal Suenens called a "surprise of the Holy Spirit."

The Catholic pentecostal movement began in Pittsburgh, Pennsylvania, at Duquesne University, a school run appropriately enough by the Holy Ghost Fathers. In 1966, two Duquesne University lay theology professors, Ralph Kiefer and Bill Storey, began a spiritual search which led them to read David Wilkerson's *The Cross and the Switchblade* and John Sherrill's *They Speak with Other Tongues.* After reading these books, the two men began a search of the Pittsburgh area for someone who had received the baptism in the Holy Ghost with the accompaniment of speaking in tongues. In time, with the help of an Episcopal priest in a Presbyterian-led prayer group, Kiefer and Storey were baptized in the Holy Spirit and spoke in languages they had never learned.[9]

These two Spirit-filled professors then made plans for a weekend retreat for several friends to seek an outpouring of the Holy Spirit in the Catholic church. About twenty professors, graduate students, and their wives gathered over the weekend of February 17-19, 1967, in Pittsburgh for the first Catholic pentecostal prayer meeting on record. The participants were asked to read the first four chapters of the Acts of the Apostles and *The Cross and the Switchblade.* The meetings were held in a large retreat house known as the Ark and the Dove, while the gathering was sponsored by a campus group called Chi Rho. In time, this gathering was dubbed "the Duquesne weekend."

The Holy Spirit hovered over the Ark and the Dove during that fantastic weekend. After an intensive study of the book of Acts, and a day devoted to prayer and study, many of the participants were anxious to seek for the baptism in the Holy Spirit. But a birthday party for one of the priests had been planned for Saturday night. As the party began, a sense of conviction and expectancy pervaded the atmosphere. Soon, one student after another slipped out of the party and went upstairs to the chapel to pray.

Strange things began to happen to these young people as they began to seek the Lord for pentecostal fullness. A student by the name of David Mangan entered the room and was suddenly "slain in the Spirit," falling prostrate on the floor. He reported the following experiences:

"I cried harder than I ever cried in my life, but I did not shed one tear. All of a sudden Jesus Christ was so real and so present that I could feel Him all around. I was overcome with such a feeling of love that I cannot begin to describe it."[10]

Later the entire group left the party downstairs and gathered in the chapel for the first totally Catholic pentecostal prayer meeting. Patricia Gallagher described the meeting in this new "upper room":

That night the Lord brought the whole group into the chapel. I found my prayers pouring forth that the others might come to know him, too. My former shyness about praying aloud was completely gone as the Holy Spirit spoke through me. The professors then laid hands on some of the students but most of us received the "Baptism in the Spirit" while kneeling before the blessed sacrament in prayer. Some of us started speaking in tongues, others received gifts of discernment, prophecy, and wisdom. But the most important gift was the fruit of love which bound the whole community together. In the Lord's spirit we found a unity we had long tried to achieve on our own.[11]

As these Catholic seekers prayed through to Pentecost, many things familiar to classical Pentecostals began to take place. Some laughed uncontrollably "in the Spirit"; while one young man rolled across the floor in ecstasy. Shouting praises to the Lord, weeping, and speaking in tongues characterized this beginning of the movement in the Catholic church. Small wonder they were called "Catholic pentecostals" by the public and the press when news spread about the strange events in Pittsburgh.[12]

The fire that was kindled in Duquesne University soon was ignited in Notre Dame University in South Bend, Indiana. This outbreak came after a letter from Ralph Kiefer stirred the interest of several student and faculty leaders who also were interested in the spiritual renewal of the church. After some investigation and initial skepticism, a group of some nine students gathered in the apartment of Bert Ghezzi and were baptized in the Holy Spirit.

However, they did not manifest any overt spiritual gifts. To get some help, they made contact with Ray Bullard, a member of the Assemblies of God and president of the South Bend chapter of the Full Gospel Businessmen. Ghezzi describes how this group of Catholic intellectuals received the gifts of tongues:

We went to Ray's house the following week and met in his basement room with eleven Pentecostal ministers and their wives from all over Indiana. They spent the evening attempting to persuade us that if you were baptized in the Spirit you had to be speaking in tongues. We let them know we were open to praying in tongues, but we held fast to our conviction that we were already baptized in the Spirit because we could see it in our lives. The issue got resolved because we were willing to speak in tongues if it were not seen as a theological necessity to being baptized in the Holy Spirit. At a certain point, we said we were willing to give it a try, and a man explained to us what was involved. Very late that evening, sometime after midnight, down in that basement room, the brothers lined us up on one side of the room and the ministers on the other side of the room, and they began to pray in tongues and to walk toward us with outstretched hands. Before they reached us, many of us began to pray and sing in tongues.

After a time of praying in tongues, Ghezzi says, the students' Pentecostal friends asked them when they would be leaving the Catholic Church and joining up with a Pentecostal church:

> The question actually left us a little shocked. Our response was that we wouldn't be leaving the Catholic Church, that being baptized in the Holy Spirit was completely compatible with our belief in the Catholic Church. We assured our friends that we had a great respect for them and that we would have fellowship with them, but we would be remaining in the Catholic Church.
>
> I think there's something significant about the fact that those of us who were baptized in the Holy Spirit then would never have thought about abandoning the Roman Catholic Church.
>
> Our Pentecostal friends had seen Catholics join Pentecostal churches when they were baptized in the Spirit. Because we did not do that, the Catholic charismatic renewal became possible.[13]

The events at Duquesne were now repeated at Notre Dame—the intellectual capital of American Catholicism. This is a description of a typical Catholic prayer meeting on campus. After much singing, praying, and Bible reading:

> ... The leader announced that it was time for anyone who so desired to be prayed over to receive the gifts of the Spirit. About half a dozen requested this, among them the two priests. After a few practical instructions about how to recognize the gift of tongues when it comes, five or six of those who had already received the baptism in the Spirit gathered in a semicircle around the first person to be prayed over. They laid their hands on his head, and started to pray, at first in English. After a few moments one of them began to speak something that sounded very much like Arabic. A moment later, another also went into another tongue, which sounded entirely different. Before long, all those who were praying over the "candidate" were praying in tongues.[14]

Campus newspapers soon began to report the incredible news of what was happening on the Notre Dame campus. The *National Catholic Reporter* picked up the story of the Notre Dame pentecost and gave the following evaluation of these events:

> There have been attempts to explain the Pentecostal movement at Notre Dame as a return to the devotional aspects of the Church. Some say that the movement attracts people with emotional problems. Still others say it creates a false community that needs constant reinforcement. And, of course, there are those who explain the whole phenomenon in terms such as "fanatic," "cracked," "off the deep end" or "nut." But the situation is not that simple.
>
> It would be so convenient to say that these Catholic Pentecostals were underfed, high-strung, groping intellectual misfits in a wholesome atmosphere of all-American

football-hood. It would be quite convenient, but it would also be quite untrue. There seems to be no one level of conformity in this group except a common experience.[15]

In fact, the new pentecostals at Notre Dame included several respected professors on the theology faculty, including Edward O'Connor and J. Massingberd Ford. Kevin Ranaghan was a teacher at nearby St. Mary's College. Others baptized in the Holy Spirit at Notre Dame who later became national leaders in the movement were Steve Clark and Ralph Martin, staff members in the national secretariat of the Cursillo movement; George Martin, a worker in adult education for the Diocese of Lansing; Paul DeCelles, a professor of Physics at Notre Dame; and a group of students including Bert Ghezzi, Jim Cavnar, Gerry Rauch, Dorothy Ranaghan, Phil O'Mara, and Kerry Koller.[16]

From this group of able and consecrated young people came the major leadership of the Catholic charismatic renewal movement. Most of them were in their twenties. Under their talented and inspired guidance, Pentecostalism began to spread like wildfire among Catholics in the United States and ultimately around the world.

The early growth of the movement was astounding. New prayer groups sprang up daily around the nation. A communications network revealed a stunning acceptance of the movement among clergy and laity alike. In a short time, the Catholic pentecostal movement was recognized as the fastest-growing movement in the church. This growth was dramatized by the international conferences that were convened annually in South Bend after 1967. Attendance at the conferences tended to triple every year for several years:[17]

1967 - 85	1971 - 4,000
1968 - 150	1972 - 12,000
1969 - 450	1973 - 22,000
1970 - 1,279	1974 - 30,000

By 1974, the movement had abandoned the term "pente-costal" in favor of the more neutral "charismatic" in order not to be confused with the older Pentecostals. By that year, estimates placed the number of prayer groups in America at 1,800 and a world total of 2,400. The number of participants around the world were estimated at 350,000. Among these were an estimated 2,000 priests who joined the movement.

Catholic pentecostalism grew not only in size but in influence during the 1970s. By 1973, at least one Cardinal, Suenens of Belgium, had not only joined the movement, but was appointed by Pope Paul VI to be his advisor concerning charismatic developments. Additionally, several American and Canadian bishops publicly identified with the charismatics. The leading American bishop to participate was Joseph McKinney, auxiliary bishop of Grand Rapids, Michigan, who became the liaison between the Catholic Charismatic Renewal Service Committee and the American bishops.

A key to the rapid development of Pentecostalism within the Catholic church was the careful theological attention that was devoted to it almost from the very beginning. The earliest theological reflections were done by the Benedictine monk and scholar, Kilian McDonnell, who in 1970 published a ground-breaking study entitled, *Catholic Pentecostalism: Problems in Evaluation.* This was an attempt to place the pentecostal experience within the context of the Catholic tradition.

Other early works which helped forge a Catholic charis-matic theology were Edward O'Connor's *The Pentecostal Movement in the Catholic Church* (1971); Kevin and Dorothy Ranaghan's *Catholic Pentecostals* (1969); J. Massingberd Ford's, *The Pentecostal Experience: A New Direction For American Catholics* (1970); and Donald Gelpi's *Pentecostalism: A Theological Viewpoint* (1971). Because of these studies, pente-costalism was received by Catholics as a phenomenon in full accord with their traditions and not as a Protestant import.

Another key to the early progress of the movement was the positive but cautious attitude of the bishops. In their 1969

"Report of the Committee on Doctrine" the bishops concluded that "theologically the movement has legitimate reasons for existence. It has a strong Biblical basis." Also
observations indicated that the participants "experienced
progress in their spiritual life," were "attracted to the reading
of Scripture," and developed "a deeper understanding of their
faith." At the end of the report, the bishops stated, "it is the
conclusion of the Committee on Doctrine that the movement
should at this point not be inhibited but allowed to develop."[18]

And develop it did! By 1975, the "latter rain" had reached
Rome itself. In an international conference held in a tent over
the ancient catacombs, over 10,000 Catholic charismatics
gathered to bring their witness to the very seat of the papacy.
At the feast of Pentecost, 1975, these spirit-filled faithful
joined a crowd of 25,000 that filled St. Peter's to hear Pope
Paul VI. Near the end of the service, the pentecostals began to
"sing in the Spirit." At the end, the organist and choir joined in
the extemporaneous singing of the "eightfold Alleluia," the
international anthem of the movement.

On Pentecost Monday, the first specifically charismatic
mass was conducted in St. Peter's with Cardinal Suenens as
celebrant. Young American charismatic leaders from Ann
Arbor, Michigan, delivered prophecies from the high altar of
the basilica. Joyful and anointed singing filled the church. In
his message to the charismatics at the end of the mass, Pope
Paul said prophetically:

How then could this "spiritual renewal" not be a "chance"
for the church and for the world? And how, in this case,
could one not take all the means to ensure that it remains so?
. . . It ought to rejuvenate the world, give it back a
spirituality, a soul, a religious thought, it ought to reopen
its closed lips to prayer and open its mouth to song, to joy,
to hymns, and to witnessing. It will be very fortuitous for

our times, for our brothers, that there should be a generation, your generation of young people, who shout out to the world the greatness of the God of Pentecost....[19]

The showers of the latter rain were truly falling in Rome!

NINE

The Cloudburst

THE SUDDEN AND UNEXPECTED APPEARANCE of Catholic pentecostalism, soon known as the "Catholic charismatic renewal," was a most significant turning point in the history of the latter-rain people. While presenting formidable theological problems, the very idea that the Roman Catholic church could tolerate and even encourage Pentecostalism gave the movement a sudden respectability that raised eyebrows in the other mainline churches. The burgeoning crowds that attended the various Catholic charismatic conferences during the 1970s sent many churchmen back to the theological drawing boards to make new assessments of the situation.

What became clear during that decade was that mainline charismatics had developed a new view of the "baptism in the Holy Spirit," which allowed Pentecostalism to flourish in the historic churches without the "cultural baggage" and rigid exclusivism espoused by the Pentecostal churches. The Wesleyan teaching of an instantaneous second experience of sanctification was not adopted by any of the new charismatic groups, although much stress was laid on holiness as the goal of the Spirit-filled Christian lifestyle. Older Pentecostals were occasionally scandalized to hear of charismatics who used tobacco, drank wine, and also spoke in tongues. Hundreds of Pentecostal pulpits vibrated with indignation at the very thought that such could be possible.

Catholic pentecostalism was even more incomprehensible to the older Pentecostals when members often claimed that their experience of the rosary, the confessional, and devotion to Mary and the church was deepened after receiving the baptism in the Holy Spirit. Because of such radical departures from commonly accepted Pentecostal views, some pastors and denominational leaders denounced the entire charismatic movement as a Satanic plot designed to replace the genuine latter rain with a diabolical counterfeit.[1]

A Charismatic Theology

Because the classical Pentecostals were either unwilling or unable to contribute to the developing charismatic theology, charismatic scholars soon developed their own new position regarding the "baptism in the Holy Spirit" which became known as the "organic view" of the experience. Prime movers in this development were Kilian McDonnell (Roman Catholic), Arnold Bittlinger (Lutheran), and Larry Christenson (Lutheran). It was presented in developed form in Larry Christenson's 1976 book *The Charismatic Renewal among Lutherans*.

Essentially, the "organic view" saw the pentecostal experience as an essential part of the "rites of initiation," i.e., baptism, confirmation, and the Eucharist. Being "baptized in the Holy Spirit" was thus identical with water baptism, while the later experiences of tongues, and other gifts of the Spirit constituted a "release" or "actualization" of the grace given and received at baptism.

This view was contrasted with the classical Pentecostal view of a separate "baptism in the Holy Ghost" subsequent to conversion and water baptism, with the necessary "initial evidence" of speaking in tongues. Though most of the new charismatics rejected the classical Pentecostal position on the necessity of tongues, they nevertheless bordered on "initial evidence." Most stated, as Christenson did, that "those who pray for the filling of the Spirit, in the context of charismatic renewal, usually speak in tongues, either at once or sometime afterwards."[2]

To avoid the idea of "two baptisms" and to adhere to the principle of "one Lord, one faith, one baptism," a person could be baptized in the Holy Spirit at his water baptism (even as an infant) while the gifts of the Spirit could appear later in his Christian experience. This view also, it was claimed, would avoid the pitfall of dividing the churches into two groups, the "spirit-filled," and the "second-class" members who had not received "the baptism."

It became common, therefore, for some charismatics to accept a "baptism in the Spirit" by faith while later seeking to "yield to tongues" not as "initial evidence" but as one of several authenticating gifts of the Spirit. Nevertheless, most charismatics felt that their experience was somehow incomplete if they failed to speak in tongues. Most of the early charismatics did speak with tongues and considered glossolalia integral to their pentecostal experience.

With new theological respectability and without the trappings of sectarian warfare, the charismatic movement entered the mainline churches in the 1970s more as a cloudburst than as a gentle shower of the latter rain. Thousands of ministers, priests, and pastors received the pentecostal experience in hopes of renewing their own spiritual lives as well as that of their parishes and even their denominations. At the grass-roots level, several million lay members of the churches received "the baptism" and decided to stay in their churches in an attempt to spread the good news among their own people.

The Jesus People

This new wave of the 1970s was also dramatically highlighted by the "Jesus People" revolution in California which spread across the nation as a youth revival. One of the first leaders in this movement was the Reverend Chuck Smith, pastor of the tiny Calvary Chapel Foursquare Church in Costa Mesa, California. The Jesus people first came to his church in the form of a dozen "hippies" who were converted and accepted into the church, to the horror of the old-line saints who failed to understand what was happening. In two frantic years, Smith was deluged with thousands of converts from the drug-oriented hippie culture who crowded into his church to find salvation and deliverance from drugs. In a few months, Smith baptized some 15,000 converts in the waters of the Pacific Ocean and was forced to move his young congregation to a tent seating 3,000 persons. By the end of the decade, Calvary Chapel built a church sanctuary seating 4,000 and counted over 25,000 in attendance at his regular Sunday services.[3]

The revival in the youth drug culture was presaged by the ministry of Dave Wilkerson. This Assemblies of God preacher left a comfortable middle-class pastorate in Philipsburg, Pennsylvania, in 1958 to minister to the young drug addicts of New York City. His ministry of deliverance to thousands of young drug addicts won the admiration of all Christians. He claimed that his "thirty second cure" for addiction, the baptism in the Holy Spirit, far surpassed the cure rates of Federal programs for hard-drug addiction.

Similar stories of mass conversions from the hippie culture spread across America during the early 1970s. Coffeehouse ministries sprang up in major cities to minister to street people. "Christian commune" ministries were opened in faraway rural areas to care for those who fled the institutional world of the traditional church. In most cases, Pentecostalism was the common denominator. It seemed to be the only spiritual force powerful enough to break the drug habit. Wherever it developed, the charismatic movement attracted masses of young people who combined the energy of the contemporary "Gospel Rock" culture, with the expressive freedom of praise and worship characteristic of the classical Pentecostals.

The mainline churches, confronted with the phenomena of this spiritual explosion, decided to attempt to conserve this "new wine" in the "old bottles" of the institutional church. Gone were the old denunciations and criticisms of "holy rollerism." Faced with huge losses of older members from their churches, mainline church leaders seemed unwilling to also write off the new converts from the hippie culture who were gravitating to the Pentecostal churches or the new independent churches which catered to the youth counter-culture. Great efforts were made to accommodate the charis-matics into the life of the churches.

The Churches Discern the Renewal

The vigor and force of the charismatic and Jesus movements forced the churches into a major reassessment of the situation. Around the world, denomination after denomination ap-pointed study commissions to report on the charismatic movement, which now seemed to have entered into every congregation in Christendom. In 1970, the United Presby-terian Church became the first major denomination to issue a comprehensive report on the movement. This became a model for the other denominational reports that followed. In produc-ing the report, the Presbyterians appointed a subcommittee made up of competent persons from the behavioral sciences to join with theologians in their study. Unlike similar studies made earlier in this century, the commission concluded that there was "no evidence of pathology in the movement." As far as tongues were concerned, the report stated that "the practice of glossolalia should neither be despised nor forbidden; on the other hand, it should not be emphasized nor made normative for Christian experience."[4]

Major studies by the Episcopal Church (1971), the Amer-ican Lutheran Church (1973), and the Lutheran Church in America (1974) were similar to the Presbyterian study of 1970. These documents also voiced concerns about possible abuses, but firmly stated that tongues-speakers could remain members of the churches in good standing.[5]

Although the roots of the renewal in some ways lay in the Methodist tradition, the United Methodist Church belatedly produced its first major evaluation of the movement in 1976. While noting that Pentecostalism had emerged from the Wesleyan tradition, the report stated that Pentecostalism "has little to do with Wesley's theology." Nevertheless, tongues-speakers were welcomed in Methodist churches, as was dramatically demonstrated in 1969 when Oral Roberts was admitted to the Boston Avenue Methodist Church in Tulsa, Oklahoma. Roberts was also admitted as a local preacher in the Oklahoma Conference by Bishop Angie Smith after promising the bishop and his thousands of "partners" that he would neither change his pentecostal theology nor his divine healing methods. The Graduate School of Theology of Oral Roberts University, headed by Methodist theologian Dr. Jimmy Buskirk, was approved by the United Methodist Church in 1982 as a seminary for the training of Methodist ministers. Beyond Methodism, ORU became the epicenter for training charismatic leaders for all the churches.[6]

The response of the American Roman Catholic hierarchy continued to be positive and supportive during the 1970s. Already noted was the 1969 report of the bishops which stated that the movement "should not be inhibited but allowed to develop." A 1975 report of the American bishops saw "positive and desirable directions" in the charismatic movement. This report also stated:

> Where the movement is making solid progress there is a strongly grounded faith in Jesus Christ as Lord. This in turn leads to a renewed interest in prayer, both private and group prayer. Many of those who belong to the movement experience a new sense of spiritual values, a heightened consciousness of the action of the Holy Spirit, the praise of God and a deepening personal commitment to Christ. Many,

too, have grown in devotion to the Eucharist and partake more fruitfully in the sacramental life of the church. Reverence for the mother of the Lord takes on fresh meaning and many feel a deeper sense of attachment to the Church.[7]

International Roman Catholic reaction to the renewal was most fully expressed in three publications known as the *Malines Documents*, issued under the authority of Leon Joseph Cardinal Leon Suenens. These documents dealt with various aspects of the renewal, as reflected in their titles: *Theological and Pastoral Orientations I* (1974), *Ecumenism II* (1978), and *Social Action* (1979). All these documents accept the validity of the renewal, reject the idea of the cessation of the charismata, and offer pastoral guidelines on how to integrate the renewal into the ongoing life of the church. In Suenen's famous phrase, the renewal was a "stream of grace" which would succeed ultimately when it had disappeared into the lifestream of the church, bringing renewal to the Body of Christ throughout the world.[8]

The most negative assessments of the renewal came from the older Holiness and fundamentalist churches that had encountered and rejected Pentecostalism earlier in the century. The Christian and Missionary Alliance, for example, reaffirmed in 1963 the "seek not — forbid not" dictum that had first been formulated by A.B. Simpson in 1907. Baptists and Nazarenes rejected the renewal out of hand, not on scriptural or theological grounds, but because Pentecostalism did not accord with their doctrines and traditions. The Lutheran Church-Missouri Synod in a 1972 report suggested that the charismatic movement was incompatible with Lutheran faith, theology, and practice.[9]

The World Council of Churches was late in issuing its position on the renewal, despite the incessant labors of David du Plessis to bring a pentecostal witness to the organization. Its report appeared in 1980. A long and detailed document that relied largely on work done in previous mainline Protestant reports, the WCC report viewed the vigorous grass-roots ecumenicity of the renewal as "a sign of hope." This was especially true for the "tired ecumenists" of the World Council, who had never been able to gather together large masses of people from the different churches on the scale that the charismatics had done. Although doubtful of the commitment of the charismatics to socio-political action, the report on the whole was positive and supportive of the spiritual and community-building aspects of the movement.[10]

In general, these study reports, while cautious and pastoral in tone, accepted the major premise of Pentecostalism, i.e. that the miraculous gifts of the Spirit did not cease after the apostolic age, but are even now demonstrated in the church by Spirit-filled believers. The major problems encountered by the churches was not related to the authenticity of the charismata in today's church, but to how these gifts could best be integrated into the life of the modern church.

The Kansas City Conference of 1977

Armed with the accumulated discernment of the churches, the charismatics turned their attention to planning several massive public gatherings during the mid-1970s to impress their message on the soul of the church and the mind of the nation. As the result of a vision shared by several charismatic and Pentecostal leaders in 1975, a call was issued in 1976 for a "general conference" of all charismatics and Pentecostals to gather in Kansas City, Missouri, in 1977 for an international, ecumenical conference which would gather together all the sectors of the renewal for the first time. The purpose of the conference was to demonstrate the unity of the movement and to make a "common witness" to the church and the world of the conference theme "Jesus is Lord."

For eighteen months an ecumenical team planned a "conference of conferences" under the leadership of Kevin Ranaghan, chairman of the Catholic Charismatic Renewal Service Committee. Under the "three streams" concept (classical Pentecostal, Protestant neo-pentecostal, and Catholic charismatic), Larry Christenson (Lutheran) and Vinson Synan (Pentecostal Holiness) served on the "executive committee" with Ranaghan. Others serving on the committee indicated the broad ecumenical base of the event. They included: Brick Bradford (Presbyterian), Ithiel Clemmons (Church of God in Christ), Howard Courtney (Church of the Foursquare Gospel), Robert Frost (Independent), Robert Hawn (Episcopal), Roy Lamberth (Southern Baptist), Nelson Litwiller (Mennonite), Bob Mumford (Independent), Ken Pagard (American Baptist), Carlton Spencer (Elim Fellowship), Ross Whetstone (Methodist), and David Stern (Messianic Jewish).

The Kansas City charismatic conference served as the climactic event in the history of the latter-rain people. For the first (and only) time, all the important groups in the entire tradition met together at the same time and at the same place. In the mornings, the different denominational groups met in separate arenas and auditoriums in the city. Included were morning sessions for Catholics, Lutherans, Presbyterians, Episcopalians, denominational Pentecostals, independent Pentecostals, Methodists, and Messianic Jews. Afternoon workshops were offered by all the groups and were open to all. In the evening, sessions for everyone from all the conferences gathered in Arrowhead Stadium for the ecumenical worship and praise services. Chairman Ranaghan proclaimed that the conference was probably the most ecumenical large gathering of Christians in 800 years.

The most powerful word to the conference came in a prophetic call to unity that brought the huge assembly to its knees in tears of repentance:[11]

Come before me, with broken hearts and contrite spirits
For the body of my Son is broken.

Come before me, with tears and mourning,
For the body of my Son is broken.

The light is dim, my people are scattered,
The body of my Son is broken.

I gave all I had in the body and blood of my Son,
It spilled on the earth.
The body of my Son is broken.

Turn from the sins of your fathers,
And walk in the ways of my Son.
Return to the plan of your Father.
Return to the purpose of your God.
The body of my Son is broken.

The Lord says to you: stand in unity with one another,
And let nothing tear you apart.
And, by no means separate from one another,
Through your jealousies and bitternesses,
And your personal preferences,
But hold fast to one another.
Because I am about to let you undergo
A time of severe trial and testing,
And you'll need to be in unity with one another.
But I tell you this also,
I am Jesus, the Victor King.
And I have promised you victory.

Symbolic of the unity called for in this prophecy was the presence of leaders from widely divergent Christian traditions who shared the same platform in Kansas City. In one memorable service, Cardinal Suenens (Roman Catholic), Thomas Zimmerman (Assemblies of God), J.O. Patterson (Church of God in Christ), and Archbishop Bill Burnett (Anglican) stood together before the vast multitude in an unprecedented demonstration of unity.[12]

Great rejoicing and celebration filled the stands as the

ecumenical multitude sang in tongues and danced before the Lord. In reporting the conference, *Time* magazine said, somewhat irreverently, "a charismatic time was had by all." The press estimated that the Kansas City crowds represented some 4 million classical Pentecostals and 5 million charismatics in the United States.[13]

To say the least, the Kansas City Conference made a tremendous impression on the American public. One observer, Jeremy Rifkin, described it as the "superbowl of the burgeoning new Charismatic movement." His description of the event in *The Changing Order* gave some of its ecumenical flavor:

> The Kansas City football stadium had never sported an event quite so unusual. Tens of thousands of Bible-carrying, hymn-singing Christians of all shades of denominations squeezed into the stands, the bleachers, and overflowed the playing field on July 21, 1977, for what turned out to be the first annual superbowl of the burgeoning new Charismatic movement. They were Catholic, Baptist, Presbyterian, Episcopalian and Methodist, all praising the Lord and embracing each other in brotherly love. Even for a casual observer of Christian religious history, such a moment of ecumenical bliss certainly gave the impression that a miracle had, indeed taken place.[14]

The most unforgettable moment of the conference came as Bob Mumford moved to the climax of his sermon in one of the evening sessions in the stadium. Lifting his Bible into the air, Mumford exclaimed, "If you sneak a peek at the back of the book, Jesus wins!" The crowd of some 50,000 roared their approval with 15 minutes of ecstatic praise and applause.[15]

Although many saw only the excitement and fervor of the meetings, others saw deeper currents of meaning in the gathering. To some, Kansas City meant resistance to the secular, materialistic culture of the times and a return to spiritual values. According to David Stump, the Kansas City charismatics were "clearly seeing the years ahead as a time of struggle to determine if the future would be formed in a Christian image or in the image of secular materialism."[16]

Kansas City in 1977 represented a cresting of the movement in America. It was the greatest and most visible sign of unity in the entire history of the latter-rain people. After Kansas City, the various denominational charismatic groups returned to their separate annual conferences. Many groups, such as the Roman Catholics, began to conduct large regional conferences which further reduced the visibility of the movement in the eyes of the media. Diversification and regionalization became the order of the day. Even so, the 15,000 Lutheran charismatics that gathered annually in Minneapolis remained the largest annual meeting of Lutherans in the country, while the 10,000 Catholics who continued to meet each year at Notre Dame remained one of the most important annual gatherings of Catholics in the United States.

Pentecost Celebrations

The diversification that followed Kansas City included the beginning of a worldwide observance of Pentecost Sunday as an ecumenical demonstration of the unity of the churches. Jointly suggested by Cardinal Suenens and Vinson Synan, these celebrations spread to many of the major cities of the world. In 1979, over 250,000 persons attended celebrations in the United States. The largest such celebration was in New York in 1979, where 35,000 persons met in Giant Stadium to celebrate the birthday of the church. Huge Pentecost celebrations were held also in cities as far removed as London and Bombay. In many cities such as Dallas and Oklahoma City, these annual ecumenical meetings have become a regular part of the local church calendar.[17]

All the foregoing events were sponsored and carried out by charismatic and Pentecostal people without the participation of those outside the movements. They helped to stamp the latter-rain people on the consciousness of the nation as a major religious and social force.

A preview of political developments occurred at the Kansas City conference when charismatic Baptist healing evangelist, Ruth Carter Stapleton, helped the charismatics to identify with the "born-again" politics of her brother, President Jimmy Carter. The president's letter which was read to the Kansas City conference not only brought the crowd to its feet, it brought presidential politics into the evangelical religious arena. This lesson was well learned by Carter's successor, Ronald Reagan, who openly courted the evangelicals and charismatics in his quest for the White House.

Washington for Jesus 1980

By 1980, the political potential of the movement was forcefully demonstrated in the "Washington for Jesus" rally which brought over 500,000 Christians to the mall in Washington for one of the largest gatherings in the history of the nation's capital. A then-unknown Pentecostal preacher, John Geminez, pastor of the Rock Church in Virginia Beach, Virginia, issued the call for this multitude to preach and pray from sunup to sunset on July 4, 1980.

The speakers did not support any candidate or political party in the 1980 election; but they loudly and unitedly spoke out against drug abuse, homosexuality, and abortion, and in favor of prayer in public schools. The candidate in 1980 whose platform most closely matched the temper of the charismatics was Ronald Reagan, although Carter's public personal Christian testimony was much closer to that of the latter-rain people. Of even more significance than the political overtones of the rally was the history-making ecumenical aspects of the event. Evangelicals and charismatics stood together publicly to demonstrate their unity on matters of vital national public policy.

The coming together of evangelicals and charismatics in Washington presaged other changes in American church life. Although little had been said by mission boards of the mainline churches, Pentecostalism had long since swept into the mission fields of their denominations. Southern Baptists whispered the rumor that an estimated 75 percent of their missionaries had spoken in tongues in the various "renovation" and charismatic movements in the third world during the 1970s. Large numbers of Methodist, Presbyterian, Anglican, and Lutheran missionaries had become practicing pentecostals on the field—a fact they did not broadcast back home.

The latter rain was also falling in the major independent seminaries of the nation as well as in many of the denominational schools. This led to a fever of research and writing on the doctoral level on all things pertaining to Pentecostalism. Literally hundreds of theses and dissertations were produced in the universities and seminaries of the world after 1970. As a result, the "Society for Pentecostal Studies" was formed in 1970 to promote and coordinate this research explosion. The SPS soon became one of the most active and vigorous theological societies in the United States.[18]

A sign of the times in the academic world was the development of the most popular course ever offered at Fuller Theological Seminary. Taught by professors John Wimber and Peter Wagner, "Signs, Wonders and Church Growth" attracted some 100 students to study the use of the gifts of the Spirit in the churches. Wimber's classes often ended with prayer for the sick, tongues, and prophecies. Wimber put his theories into practice in his "Vineyard Christian Fellowship" congregation in Yorba Linda, California where 4,000 persons attended Sunday worship services in a church that by 1982 was only five years old.[19]

As large numbers of young converts from the "Jesus

movement" felt the call to preach, they increasingly entered seminaries and schools of theology to prepare for the ministry. By 1983, about one-third of the student bodies of Fuller and Gordon-Conwell seminaries were made up of Pentecostals or charismatics. Many of these graduates were called to serve traditional mainline congregations as pastors, musicians, and ministers of Christian education. By the 1980s they were being welcomed with open arms and with few questions asked about their charismatic experiences.

TEN

Three Streams— One River

THE GREAT ARMY OF YOUNG "Jesus people" who were accepted into the ministry of the mainline churches constituted a bridgehead of Spirit-filled ministers and priests who were destined to bring on the next phase of the movement. Since most of these young enthusiasts were not raised in classical Pentecostal homes, they felt few ties to the older Pentecostal denominations although they spoke in tongues and enthusiastically espoused pentecostal practices.

Some of them founded new congregations and even denominations which were fully pentecostalized, but which were not labeled either Pentecostal or charismatic. Often the articles of faith of these groups could not be distinguished from any of the mainline evangelical bodies. The Maranatha campus ministries of Bob Weiner and his associates, for example, were pentecostal in worship and experience although nothing in the official doctrinal statements would distinguish them from the average evangelical denomination.

Untold numbers of similar young ministers entered the ministries of Baptist, Lutheran, Methodist, and Presbyterian churches. The same story was true of the Roman Catholic and Eastern Orthodox churches. Great numbers of young people with a spiritual formation in the charismatic movement entered the seminaries of the churches without any specific labels to distinguish them from other candidates for the priesthood. These young people became the vanguard for the next chapter in the story of the latter rain people.

A Third Wave

By 1983, some leaders were talking about a "third wave" of Pentecostalism which would enter the mainline churches with little struggle or notoriety. This "third wave" would be a successor to the first two, i.e. the classical Pentecostals and the charismatics. The new wave would be made up of evangelicals in the major traditional churches who would receive and exercise the gifts of the Spirit without accepting the labels. Peter Wagner of Fuller Theological Seminary is such a man. He speaks in tongues but refuses to call himself a pentecostal or a charismatic. In explaining the "third wave," Wagner stated:

> I see in the 80's an opening of the straightline evangeli-cals and other Christians to the supernatural work of the Holy Spirit that the Pentecostals and Charismatics have experienced, but without becoming either Charismatic or Pentecostal.[1]

Using his own experience as an example, Wagner further elaborated on the future of the "third wave" people:

> I see myself as neither a Charismatic nor a Pentecostal. I belong to the Lake Avenue Congregational Church. I'm a Congregationalist. My church is not a charismatic church, although some of our members are charismatic. There is a charismatic prayer group that meets on Monday nights in a home.
> However, our church is more and more open to the same

way that the Holy Spirit does work among Charismatics. For example, our pastor gives an invitation after every service (we have three services on Sunday morning) for people who need physical healing and inner healing to come forward and go to the prayer room and be anointed with oil and prayed for, and we have teams of people who know how to pray for the sick.

We like to think that we are doing it in a congregational way; we're not doing it in a charismatic way. But we're getting the same results. I myself have several major theological differences with Pentecostals and Charismatics, which don't mar any kind of mutual ministry, but keep me from saying I'm a charismatic.[2]

By the mid 1980s there was evidence that the "third wave" was indeed entering the mainline churches without the confusion of labels that had caused such great problems in the past. A symbol of the new attitudes that were developing among evangelicals were the striking views of Harold Lind-sell, well-known theologian and former editor of *Christianity Today*. In his 1983 book, *The Holy Spirit in the Latter Days*, Lindsell said:

We have been talking about the glorious work of the Holy Spirit in the lives of God's people. It should be apparent to all that I accept as a fact that some of God's people are filled or baptized with the Holy Spirit, and that nomenclature is purely a secondary matter that should not keep us from appropriating what lies behind differing terms for the same experience. It is also a fact that God, through His Spirit, does perform miracles and healings. Speaking in tongues does happen and is a bona fide gift of the Spirit. There are a few people of God here and there who receive gifts of healing or miracles. These gifts have not ceased. They are still there even though they occur with less frequency than some people suppose.[3]

Lindsell's credentials as an evangelical leader are impeccable. If his thinking is typical of a large proportion of mainline evangelicals, there would seem to be nothing to stop a spiritual tidal wave from pouring through the traditional churches.

A major reason for the existence of the pentecostal/charismatic movements and the new "third wave" movement in the mainline churches is a great hunger for more expressive worship among most Christians. This emotional need is obviously not being satisfied by the liturgies and rituals of the historic churches. In a major study done in Minnesota in 1983, Christians of the mainline churches demonstrated what Martin Marty called a "pick and choose" attitude toward their faith.[4]

About 90 percent of the respondents preferred a "free-form" type of communication with God, in preference to the stylized and ritualized forms of traditional worship and prayer. The majority of the Minnesota respondents were Lutherans and Roman Catholics. The desire for direct and free communication with a God who "intervenes in their lives and directs them in their vocations" leads many of them to participate in Pentecostal and charismatic prayer and worship services.[5]

Where the churches are not meeting this need, the people are voting with their feet. By 1983, a major concern of many charismatic leaders in the Catholic and mainline Protestant churches was the increasing numbers of charismatic laypersons who were leaving the churches and joining local Pentecostal or independent charismatic churches.

The "third wave" may represent the reaction of the churches to this felt need. As more churches open up to freer and more "charismatic" worship, fewer church members are likely to desert their local churches. In time, as the Pentecostal churches moderate some of their more extreme practices, and the mainline churches open up to more freedom in exercising the gifts of the Spirit, the differences between them are likely to diminish.

In 1983, Richard Quebedeaux published an updated revision of his earlier book entitled, *The New Charismatics*. The subtitle of his new book describes what has happened to the charismatic renewal in recent years. It is "how a Christian renewal movement became part of the American religious mainstream." Quebedeaux believes that, by the end of the 1970s, Pentecostalism had achieved its primary goal—"that of making the once-despised pentecostal experience acceptable within mainline Protestantism and Catholicism." Thereafter "there was no longer any need for its continued existence *as a movement*." It could then merge into the mainstream churches without a particular separate identity. By the late 1970s the charismatic movement "had run out of steam" according to Quebedeaux, "but not out of abiding significance."[6]

Throughout the history of the latter-rain people, similar pronouncements have been made during periods of relative quiet and subdued revival fervor. But, always, an even stronger wave of Pentecostalsim ensued. The rising ministries of a new generation of evangelists in America, including Jimmy Swaggart, Kenneth Copeland, and the pentecostally-inclined Southern Baptist James Roberson, indicate that the sawdust trail will still be with us for years to come. Also the rising star of Reinhardt Bonnke in South Africa with his gospel tent seating 35,000 shows that the pentecostal message still relates powerfully to the struggling masses of the Third World. Thousands of unknown classical Pentecostal evangelists continue to spread the word to the humble and forgotten peoples of the world.

Three Streams—One River

For thirty years, church leaders have recognized that Pentecostalism had become one of the three major divisions of Christianity. The idea was first mentioned by Lesslie Newbigin of South India in his 1953 book entitled, *The Household of God*. In this pioneering work, Bishop Newbigin saw three major types of Christianity in the world, each with an authentic contribution to make to the Body of Christ. According to Newbigin, the first was the Catholic tradition which emphasized continuity, orthodoxy, and the importance of the sacraments to the life of the church. The Protestant tradition, on the other hand, emphasized the centrality of the scriptures and the importance of the proclaimed word of God. The Pentecostals added to these first two historic expressions of the faith an emphasis on the present action of the Spirit in the church through the gifts of the Holy Spirit. According to Newbigin, the church needed all three emphases in order to be a powerful force in the modern world.[7] This same thought was carried forward forward by Van Dusen, as mentioned earlier.[8]

The same point was made also by Ralph Martin, a leader from the earliest days in the Catholic charismatic renewal. In his 1976 book, *Fire on the Earth*, Martin saw the charismatic renewal as the Lord's vehicle of bringing these "three streams" together. In Martin's view, the charismatic movement was the only force that could weld these forces together for a unified Christian witness.[9]

Powerful testimony to this concept in the life of one individual was given in 1979 in the autobiographical book by Michael Harper entitled *Three Sisters*. An early leader in the Anglican charismatic movement in England, Harper stated that:

> One sister (evangelical) taught me that the basis of Christian life is a personal relationship with Jesus Christ. A second (pentecostal) helped me experience the spiritual dynamic of the Holy Spirit. Yet another (Catholic) ushered me into a whole new world where I began to see the implications of Christian community.[10]

By 1984, Episcopal charismatic renewal leaders could refer to their church as follows: "Episcopal Church: Catholic-evangelical-charismatic." According to Bruce Rose:

What we are is a church which has attempted to preserve in its teaching and worship the best of Catholic tradition, while remaining open to learning from others. In the sixteenth century this meant learning a renewed reverence for and love of the Word of God from the Evangelical Protestant reformers. In the twentieth it has meant learning of the empowerment of the Holy Spirit available today as in the days of the Apostles, from the "pentecostal" churches such as the Assemblies of God. Yes, we have changed, and hopefully we will go on changing as we continue to learn and grow in the ways of our Lord Jesus Christ until that day when we shall all truly be one in Him.[11]

Indeed, by 1984, there were signs that the Episcopal church was finally ending its long period of declining numbers and entering a period of growth. This growth, many believed, was being led by the army of young charismatic pastors who were coming to the fore in the church. Of 7,200 Episcopal parishes in the United States, about 400 were experiencing charismatic renewal. Many were openly experiencing the gifts of the Spirit in their regular services. In addition, by 1984 no less than 47 percent of all the world's Anglican bishops were baptized in the Spirit and openly espousing the charismatic renewal.

Making news were parishes in Houston and Dallas, Texas; Darien, Connecticut; and Fairfax, Virginia. Others, such as St. Phillip's Cathedral in Atlanta (largest Episcopal parish in the United States), conducted regular charismatic prayer and praise rallies, separate from the regular services which attracted hundreds of enthusiastic worshippers. Of special note were three Northern Virginia parishes (Falls Church, Truro, and Church of the Apostles) which experienced phenomenal growth after choosing "to go the charismatic route."

One of these, The Church of the Apostles in Fairfax, described as an "exuberant charismatic parish," grew from 50 to over 2,000 in attendance in about seven years. At Truro, thiry-six shepherding groups meet weekly under lay leadership for Bible study and spiritual growth. The three pastors speak of their experience as: "Three streams, one river: Protestant (Bible based), Catholic (liturgical and sacramental), and pentecostal (Spirit-filled). . . all three indispensable to a thriving church."[12]

The story of these Episcopal churches is only one example of a trend that is affecting churches in most denominations around the world. At one and the same time, churches from many varied backgrounds seem to be combining these three elements to form a new type of church which just may be the shape of the future for Christendom. Because of the extensive ecumenical contacts brought about by the charismatic renewal, there is a growing appreciation for the strengths of the three streams and a spirit of sharing the treasures that have been given to each tradition by the Lord.

It has been suggested that Ezekiel's vision of the dry bones describes the way God has brought the church to renewal in the last four centuries (Ezekiel 37). The dry bones represented the church at the depths of the dark ages which greatly needed renewal. Yet, the skeleton maintained the basic sacramental and liturgical structures of the faith. The flesh and sinews which were added to the bones represented the Protestant Reformation through which the scriptures and the proclamation of the word of God put new form to the bodies. But, they still lacked the breath of the Spirit. The Pentecostal renewal brought the old bodies back to life and made them into a great living, marching army.

Of Pilgrims, Settlers, and the Landed Aristocracy

Someone has said that the first generation of a religious movement is made up of the "pilgrims" who leave their secure and comfortable homes to carve out a new home in a harsh and forbidding land. They are the revolutionaries who abandon everything to follow a new ideal. The second generation becomes the settlers who domesticate the land, build fences, and bring the basic elements of law and order to the new society. The third generation, however, evolves into the landed aristocracy. These become the arbiters of civilization, the economic barons, and the vested interests who, above all, seek to prevent any more new pilgrims or settlers from entering the land.

By the mid 1980s, it could be said that the three streams fit into the foregoing categories, at least chronologically. The classical Pentecostals were well into the third generation, and in some quarters had become the "landed aristocracy" of the latter-rain people. The Protestant neo-pentecostals were entering into the second generation and were becoming "settlers" in the evangelical world. The Catholic charismatics, however, were still "pilgrims" carving out a home in the world of the Roman Catholic church.

The major problem facing all of these streams was to maintain the revolutionary fervor of the latter rain until it could be said that the churches had truly been renewed. Many of the more optimistic leaders of the 1960s and 1970s learned that the process of renewal was a long and arduous task that would not be accomplished overnight.

Beyond the renewal of the churches is an aspect of the movement that few latter-rain people have confronted—that of transforming society. By the end of the 1970s, no group in America had a greater opportunity to challenge the existing order. With its vast armies of committed followers from all denominations, with its overwhelming faith and ardor, and with its able leadership, the charismatic movement was in a position to change America's lifestyle.

In 1979, Jeremy Rifkin stated that "today's Charismatics are providing the most significant challenge to the truths of the expansionary era yet mounted. Faith healing, speaking in tongues and prophesying are, indeed weapons of rebellion against the authority of the modern age.[13]

Seeing the charismatics as "a new liberating force," Rifkin put much faith in the latter-rain people as agents of positive change. As to the possibilities of future change, he stated:

> While it is too early to tell which way the Charismatic movement will eventually lean, a great deal will depend on their understanding of the nature of our secular-materialist culture. If they see the problem simply as one of saving fallen individuals from an evil world, leaving the institutional basis of materialism untouched, then it is likely the existing order will change them, rather than they it. If, however, the evangelical participants in the new awakening are able to introduce a Biblical notion of fallen "powers and principalities" as a dual concern along with individual renewal, then this new awakening may, indeed, combine liberation with covenant and change the course of history.[14]

The Future of the Latter Rain

In the light of many studies that have been made in the past and projections for the future, it is possible to look ahead to see what is in store for the latter-rain people. According to projections made by the World Council of Churches in the early 1970s, by the year 2000 A.D. over 50 percent of all the Christians in the world will be: 1) non-white; 2) from the Southern Hemisphere; and 3) of the pentecostal or charismatic variety. Events and church growth patterns of the past several years seem to confirm these trends.

If these projections hold until the end of the century, it is not beyond reason to predict that Christendom at that time could very well approximate the following configuration:

Twenty-five percent will be classical Pentecostals, coming predominately from the burgeoning pentecostal movements in the Third World. These Christians will continue to have a minimum of liturgy and ritual and will emphasize the gifts of the Holy Spirit in their regular services. They will continue to be the fastest-growing churches in the world. Many "super churches" will emerge in third world nations as well as in the United States.

Twenty-five percent will be charismatic Christians in the mainline Protestant and Catholic churches. These will come mainly from the developed Western nations in Europe and North America. Their services will be mildly charismatic and will be typical of the "third wave" type of Christian who may or may not carry the label pentecostal or charismatic. They will gradually surpass the old "liberal" churches in size and influence. In a sense, they will become the "mainline" churches of the twenty-first century.

Twenty-five percent will be non-charismatic Christians from the mainline Protestant and Catholic churches. These will include two groups; the "liberal" churches which will continue to decline in numbers, and the non-charismatic evangelical churches which will continue to grow, but which will become a smaller proportion of the total number of Christians. The "liberals" will have less power in the denominational structures, but will continue to dominate the ecumenical movement. The "evangelicals" will withdraw all approval of the charismatic movement and more and more withdraw into a defensive fundamentalist shell.

Twenty-five percent will be nominal Christians from all the churches who do not practice their faith and are Christians only in a cultural sense. Most of these will be in a progressive condition of apostasy and will be Christians only in the faintest historical or cultural sense. They will constitute the vast number of Western (mostly white) church members who find the church irrelevant to modern man, and will, as apostates, leave their names on the church rolls while seldom if ever attending services, or leave the church entirely.

It is altogether possible that the future of Christianity will be molded by the developing Third-World, indigenous, pentecostal churches interreacting with the vigorous charismatic elements in the traditional churches. The recent history of church growth in Africa and Latin America indicate that Christian affairs of the twenty-first century may well be largely in the hands of the surging national pentecostal churches of the Third World and a resurgent Roman Catholicism inspired and renewed by the charismatic renewal.

Whether or not this scenario takes place is a matter for future scholars to confirm or deny. One thing that is certain, however, is that the latter rain will continue to fall until the end of the age.

> Therefore be patient, brothers, until the coming of the Lord. See how the farmer waits for the precious fruit of the earth, waiting patiently for it until it receives the early and latter rain.
>
> You also be patient. Establish your hearts, for the coming of the Lord is at hand (Jas 5:7-8).

Notes

Chapter Two
The Latter-Rain People

1. David Barrett, *World Christian Encyclopedia* (London, 1982), pp. 1-104.
2. Peter Wagner, "The Greatest Church Growth is Beyond our Shores," *Christianity Today*, May 18, 1984, pp. 25-31.
3. Richard Ostling in "Counting Every Soul on Earth," *Time*, May 3, 1982, pp. 66-67. The subgroupings under "Protestant" are not inclusive.
4. Barrett, *Encyclopedia*. pp. 815-848.
5. Ibid., p. 838.
6. Kenneth Kantzer, "The Charismatics among Us," *Christianity Today*, February 22, 1980, pp. 25-29.
7. Ibid.
8. Constance Jacquet, *Yearbook of American and Canadian Churches* (Nashville, 1983), p. 225.
9. Ibid., p. 226.
10. Elmer Towns, "The World's Ten Largest Churches," *Christian Life*, January 1983, pp. 60-66.
11. Ibid.

Chapter Three
The Gathering Clouds

1. Henry P. Van Dusen, "Third Force in Christendom," *Life*, June 9, 1958, pp. 113-124.
2. "But What About Hicks?" *Christian Century*, July 7, 1954, pp. 814-815. Also see Tommy Hicks, *Millions Found Christ* (Los Angeles, 1956).
3. Charles Sydnor, Jr., "The Pentecostals," *Presbyterian Survey*, May 1964, pp. 30-32; June 1964, 36-39.
4. Quoted in Warren Lewis, *Witnesses to the Holy Spirit* (Valley Forge, Penn. 1978), p.121.
5. Ibid., p. 122.
6. Phillip Schaff, *Nicene and Post-Nicene Fathers* (Grand Rapids, 1956), XII, pp. 168-170.
7. Quoted in Lewis, *Witnesses*, p. 173.
8. Ernest R. Sandeen, *The Roots of Fundamentalism: British and American*

Millenarianism, *1800-1930*, (Chicago: 1970), p. 7.

9. Ibid., pp. 26-36.

10. William S. Merricks, *Edward Irving, the Forgotten Giant* (East Peoria, Illinois, 1983), pp. 179-180. Also see Jean Christie Root, *Edward Irving, Man, Preacher, Prophet* (Boston, 1912), pp. 70-112.

11. Thomas Carlyle, *Reminiscences* (New York, 1881), p. 58.

12. Gordon Strachan, *The Pentecostal Theology of Edward Irving* (London, 1973), pp. 193-201; Also see Larry Christenson, *A Message to the Charismatic Movement* (East Weymouth, Mass., 1972) and "Pentecostalism's Forgotten Forerunner," in Vinson Synan, *Aspects of Pentecostal-Charismatic Origins* (Plainfield, N.J., 1975), pp. 15-37.

13. Charles H. Spurgeon, *Spurgeon's Sermons* (Grand Rapids, Michigan, reprint from 1857), I, pp. 129-130.

14. William Arthur, *The Tongue of Fire* (Columbia, S.C., 1891), pp. 288, 315, 375-376.

15. Ibid., p. 376.

16. Vinson Synan, *Holiness-Pentecostal Movement in the United States* (Grand Rapids, Michigan, 1971), p. 37.

17. Donald Dayton, "From Christian Perfection to the Baptism of the Holy Ghost," Synan, *Aspects*, pp. 39-54.

18. Ibid. p. 46.

19. Ibid. p. 47.

20. Ibid.

21. Martin Wells Knapp, *Lightning Bolts from Pentecostal Skies, or the Devices of the Devil Unmasked* (Cincinnati: 1898).

22. Melvin E. Dieter, *The Holiness Revival of the Nineteenth Century* (Metuchen, N.J., 1980) p. 245. Also see Dieter, "Wesleyan-Holiness Aspects of Pentecostal Origins," comp. Synan, *Aspects*, p. 67.

23. Timothy Smith, *Called Unto Holiness* (Kansas City, 1962), p. 25.

24. Reuben A. Torrey, *The Person and Work of the Holy Spirit* (New York: Fleming H. Revell Company, 1910), pp. 176-210.

25. Richard K. Curtis, *They Called Him Mister Moody* (Garden City, New York, 1962), pp. 149-150.

26. Edward O'Connor, "Hidden Roots of the Charismatic Renewal in the Catholic Church," comp. Synan, *Aspects,* pp. 169-192.

Chapter Four
The Rain Falls in America

1. Torrey, *Baptism in the Holy Ghost* (London: James Nisbet & Co. Ltd. 1895), p. 16.

2. Ibid.

3. Andrew Murray, *The Full Blessing of Pentecost* (New York, 1905), pp. 28-39.

4. A.B. Simpson, *The Holy Spirit or Power from on High* (Harrisburg, Pennsylvania, 1896), pp. 93-97.

5. Dayton, "From Christian Perfection," p. 14.

6. Ibid., p. 15.

7. *Discipline of the Pentecostal Holiness Church-1901* (Dunn, N.C., 1901).
8. J. Roswell Flower, "Birth of the Pentecostal Movement," *Pentecostal Evangel*, November 26, 1950, p. 3.
9. Sarah E. Parham, *The Life of Charles F. Parham* (Joplin, Missouri, 1930), pp. 52-53.
10. Ibid., pp. 53-80.
11. Frank Bartleman, *How "Pentecost" Came to Los Angeles* (Los Angeles, 1925), p. 64.
12. Phineas Bresee, "The Gift of Tongues," *The Nazarene Messenger*, December 13, 1906, p. 6.
13. Alma White, *Demons and Tongues* (Bound Brook, New Jersey, 1910), p. 82.
14. Bartleman, *How Pentecost Came*, p. 60; Leonard Lovett, "Black Origins of the Pentecostal Movement," comp. Synan, *Aspects*, pp. 123-142.
15. See Synan, *Holiness-Pentecostal Movement*, pp. 117-140.
16. Ibid.
17. William W. Menzies, *Anointed to Serve: The Story of the Assemblies of God* (Springfield, Missouri, 1971), pp. 80-105.
18. Charles E. Jones, *A Guide to the Study of the Holiness Movement* (Metuchen, New Jersey, 1974), pp. 106-108; 521-522; Constance Jacquet, *Yearbook* p. 226.
19. Jacquet, *Yearbook,* pp. 225-232.

Chapter Five
The Rain Falls Around the World

1. Thomas Ball Barratt, *When the Fire Fell* (Oslo, 1927), pp. 99-126.
2. Stanley Frodsham, *With Signs Following* (Springfield, Missouri, 1946), pp. 71-72.
3. Willis C. Hoover, *Historia del Avivamiento Pentecostal de Chile* (Valparaiso, 1948); Peter Wagner, *Look Out, The Pentecostals Are Coming* (Carol Stream, Illinois, 1973), pp. 16-18.
4. Hoover, *Avivamiento en Chile*, pp. 1-36.
5. Ignacio Vergara, *El Protestantismo en Chile* (Santiago, 1962), pp. 110-111.
6. Wagner, *Look Out,* pp. 17-18.
7. Ibid., p. 18.
8. Vinson Synan, "World's Largest Congregation: a Cathedral in Chile," *Christianity Today* January 17, 1975, pp. 33-34.
9. Victor Monterosso, William Reed, and Harmon Johnson, *Latin American Church Growth* (Grand Rapids, 1969), pp. 100-107.
10. Walter Hollenweger, *The Pentecostals: The Charismatic Movement in the Churches* (Minneapolis, 1972), pp. 75-76 ; Daniel Berg, *Enviado Por Deus: Memorias de Daniel Berg* (Sao Paulo, AdD 1959), passim.
11. Hollenweger, *The Pentecostals*, pp. 76-79; Wagner, *Look Out*, pp. 24-25
12. Barrett, *World Christian Encyclopedia*, pp. 186-195.
13. Wagner, *Look Out*, pp. 25; 116.
14. Monterosso, Reed, and Johnson, *Latin American Church Growth,* p. 58

15. Peter Wagner, *Your Spiritual Gifts Can Make Your Church Grow* (Ventura, California, 1979), pp. 11-30.
16. Wagner, *Look Out,* p. 25.
17. Joseph Anfuso and David Sczepanski, *He Gives, He Takes Away* (Eureka, California, 1983).
18. Steve Durasoff, *Bright Wind of the Spirit* (Englewood Cliffs, New Jersey, 1972), pp. 220-221.
19. Ibid., p. 222.
20. Ibid., p. 223.
21. Steve Durasoff, *Pentecost Behind the Iron Curtain* (Plainfield, New Jersey, 1972), pp. 17-22. Peter Varonaev (son of Ivan Varonaev), interview with the author, February 17, 1984, Toppenish, Washington.
22. Durasoff, *Bright Wind,* p. 234.
23. John T. Nichol, *Pentecostalism* (New York, 1966), pp. 193-198.
24. Joel A. McCollam, "O Lord, We're Free at Last," *Charisma*, October 1983, pp. 40-46.

Chapter Six
The Rain Rejected

1. William Willoughly, "Tongues Speaking Gains Prestige," *Logos*, April, 1974, pp. 59-60.
2. Bartleman, *How Pentecost Came*, p. 54.
3. Ibid; Synan, *Holiness Pentecostal Movement*, p. 95.
4. Oral Roberts, *My Story* (Tulsa, 1961), p. 134.
5. White, *Demons and Tongues*, pp. 43, 56, 71-83, 82.
6. Horace Ward, "The Anti-Pentecostal Argument," comp. Synan, *Aspects*, p. 104. Also see Louis S. Bauman, *The Modern Tongues Movement Examined and Judged* (Long Beach, 1941), p. 1.
7. H.J. Stolee, *Speaking in Tongues* (Minneapolis, 1963), p. 112.
8. Synan, *Holiness-Pentecostal Movement*, p.144.
9. Ibid.
10. Benjamin B. Warfield, *Counterfeit Miracles* (Carlisk, Pa., 1918), p. 21.
11. Synan, *Holiness-Pentecostal Movement*, pp. 206-207.
12. Alexander Mackie, *The Gift of Tongues: A Study in the Pathological Aspects of Christianity* (New York, 1921), pp. 254-266, 275.
13. George Bernard Cutten, *Speaking with Tongues Historically and Psychologically Considered* (New Haven, 1927), passim.
14. Kilian McDonnell, *Charismatic Renewal and the Churches* (New York, 1976), pp. 1-16.

Chapter Seven
The Rain Reconsidered

1. Menzies, *Anointed to Serve*, pp. 182-227.
2. Oral Roberts, *My Story* (Tulsa, Oklahoma, privately printed, 1961) passim.

3. Vinson Synan, *The Old-Time Power: A History of the Pentecostal Holiness Church* (Franklin Springs, Georgia, 1973), pp. 220-274.

4. David Harrell, *All Things Are Possible: The Healing and Charismatic Revivals in Modern America* (Bloomington, Indiana, 1975), pp. 225-238.

5. Demos Shakarian, *The Happiest People on Earth* (Old Tappan, New Jersey, 1975).

6. Hollenweger, *The Pentecostals*, pp. 6-7.

7. Durasoff, *Bright Wind*, pp. 145-165.

8. Michael Harper, *As at the Beginning: The Twentieth Century Pentecostal Revival* (London, 1965), p. 51.

9. David du Plessis, *The Spirit Bade Me Go: The Astounding Move of God in the Denominational Churches* (Oakland, California, 1961), pp. 9-29.

10. David du Plessis, *A Man Called Mr. Pentecost: David du Plessis As Told to Bob Slosser* (Plainfield, New Jersey, 1977).

11. David du Plessis, "Newsletter," February - March 1984, p. 2.

12. Gerald Derstine, *Following the Fire* (Plainfield, New Jersey, 1980), pp. 83-165.

13. Mc Donnell, *Presence, Power, Praise*, I, pp. 10-20.

14. Dennis Bennett, *Nine O'Clock in the Morning* (Plainfield, New Jersey, 1970); Also see Sherrill, *They Speak with Other Tongues*, pp. 61-6

15. Bennett, *Nine O'Clock*, p. 15.

16. Ibid., pp. 20-21.

17. Ibid., p. 61.

18. Ibid., pp. 61-72.

19. *Time* August 15, 1960, pp. 52-55.

20. *Newsweek*, July 4, 1960, p. 77.

21. Dennis Bennett, Personal Interview with the author. Kansas City, July, 1977.

22. Sherrill, *They Speak*, p. 61.(Quoting *Living Church*, July 17, 1960)

23. *Time*, March 29, 1963, p. 52.

24. Ibid.

25. Frank Farrell, "Outburst of Tongues: The New Penetration," *Christianity Today*, September 13, 1963, pp. 3-7.

26. Ibid.

27. *Time*, May 17, 1963, p. 84.

28. *Time*, August 15, 1960, p. 55.

29. Larry Christenson, *The Charismatic Renewal among Lutherans* (Minneapolis: 1976), pp. 1-31. Also: Larry Christenson, personal interview with author, (Rome, Italy), 1975.

Chapter Eight
The Rain Falls on Catholics

1. See David F. Wells, *Revolution in Rome* (Downers Grove, Illinois, 1972).

2. Kilian Mc Donnell and Arnold Bittlinger, *The Baptism in the Holy Spirit as an Ecumenical Problem* (South Bend, Indiana, 1972, pp. 29-30). Also see Mc Donnell's *Catholic Pentecostalism: Problems in Evaluation* (Pecos, New Mexico, 1970).

3. O'Connor, "The Hidden Roots," pp. 169-192.
4. Ibid., p. 177.
5. Yves Congar, *Chrétiens Désunis*, (1937).
6. O'Connor, "Hidden Roots," pp. 183-188.
7. Ibid., pp. 185-186.
8. Ibid. See also Francis Sullivan, *Charisms and Charismatic Renewal* (Ann Arbor, 1982), pp. 9-15.
9. Kevin and Dorothy Ranaghan, *The Catholic Pentecostal Movement* (Paramus, New Jersey, 1969), pp. 6-16; see also O'Connor, *The Pentecostal Movement in the Catholic Church*, pp. 39-43 see also *New Covenant*, February 1973,
10. Ranaghan, *The Catholic Pentecostal Movement*, p. 26.
11. Ibid., p. 35.
12. O'Connor, *Pentecostal Movement in the Catholic Church*, pp.31-35. Also see, Paul Gray, *New Covenant*, February 1973, p.8.
13. Personal Interview with Bert Ghezzi.
14. Ranaghan, *The Catholic Pentecostal Movement*, pp. 38-57.
15. Ibid., p. 38.
16. Ralph Martin, *Hungry for God* (New York, 1974), pp. 10-20.
17. O'Connor, *The Pentecostal Movement in the Catholic Church*, pp. 99-102.
18. Mc Donnell, *Presence, Power, Praise* I, pp. 207-210.
19. Ibid., III, pp. 70-76; *New Covenant*, July 1975, pp. 23-25.

Chapter Nine
The Cloudburst

1. Ray Hughes, "A Traditional Pentecostal Looks at the New Pentecostals" *Christianity Today*, June 7, 1974, pp. 6-10; also Russell Spittler, *Perspectives on the New Pentecostalism* (Grand Rapids, Michigan, Baker Book House), 1976.
2. Christenson, *Charismatic Renewal among Lutherans*, p. 48. See also Quebedeaux, *The New Charismatics*, II, pp. 127-192.
3. Quebedeaux, Ibid., pp. 130, 230-231. See also Ed Plowman, *The Jesus Movement in America* (Cool, 1971); Pat King, *The Jesus People Are Coming* (Plainfield, New Jersey, Logos Press, 1971); *Time*, August 3, 1970, pp. 31-32.
4. Mc Donnell, *Presence, Power, Praise*, I, pp. 207-210, 221-281.
5. Ibid., pp. 369-373, 547-566.
6. Ibid., II, pp. 270-290.
7. Ibid., II. pp. 104-113 (See p. 108).
8. Ibid., III, pp. 13-69, 82-174, 291-357.
9. Ibid., I, pp. 63-69, 219-220, II, pp. 114-115.
10. Ibid., III, pp. 358-372.
11. *New Covenant*, February 1978, p. 6.
12. David Manuel, *Like a Mighty River* (Orleans, Massachusetts, 1977), pp. 137-147.

13. *Time*, August 8, 1977, p. 43.
14. Jeremy Rifkin with Ted Howard, *The Emerging Order: God in the Age of Scarcity* (New York, 1979), pp. 177-178.
15. Ibid., p. 166
16. David X. Stump, "Charismatic Renewal: Up to Date in Kansas City," *America*, September 24, 1977, p. 166.17. Leon Joseph Cardinal Suenens, *Ecumenism and Charismatic Renewal: Theological and Pastoral Orientations: Malines Document II* (Ann Arbor, 1978), pp. 86-87. See also McDonnell, *Presence, Power, Praise*, III, pp. 170-171.
18. Quebedeaux, *New Charismatics*, II, pp. 82, 188, 208.
19. David Allen Hubbard, "Hazarding the Risks," *Christian Life*, October 1982, pp. 18-26.

Chapter Ten
Three Streams—One River

1. Peter Wagner, "A Third Wave?" *Pastoral Renewal*, VIII, no. 1, (July-August 1983), pp. 1-5.
2. Ibid., pp. 3-4.
3. Harold Lindsell, "My Search For the Truth About the Holy Spirit," *Christian Life*, September 1983, p. 29.
4. Kenneth L. Woodward, "Pick and Choose Christianity," *Newsweek*, September 19, 1983, pp. 82-83.
5. *Faith and Ferment* (Minneapolis: Augsburg Press and Liturgical Press 1983). This book was published simultaneously by Augsburg Press (Lutheran), and the Liturgical Press (Roman Catholic).
6. Quebedeaux, *The New Charismatics*, II, p. 239.
7. Leslie Newbigin, *The Household of God* (New York, 1954).
8. Van Dusen, "The Third Force," *Life*, pp. 113-124.
9. Ralph Martin, *Fire on the Earth* (Ann Arbor, 1976), pp. 30-42.
10. Michael Harper, *Three Sisters* (Wheaton, Illinois, 1979), pp. 9-15.
11. Bruce L. Rose, "Episcopal Church: Catholic-Evangelical-Charismatic," *Acts 29*, February 1984, pp. 1-6.d
12. Beth Spring, "Spiritual Renewal Brings Booming Growth to Three Episcopal Churches in Northern Virginia," *Christianity Today*, January 13, 1984, pp. 38-39.
13. Rifkin and Howard, *The Emerging Order*, p. 231.
14. Ibid., p. 231.

Bibliography

Primary Sources

Arthur, William, *The Tongue of Fire, or the Power of Christianity*. Columbia, S.C.: L.L. Pickett, 1891.

Barratt, Thomas Ball, *When the Fire Fell*. Oslo, Norway: Hansen and Soner, 1927.

Bartleman, Frank, *How "Pentecost" Came to Los Angeles*. Los Angeles: Privately printed, 1925. Reprinted with introduction and appendices by Vinson Synan by Logos Publications in Plainfield, N.J. in 1980 under the title *Azusa Street*.

Bauman, Louis S., *The Modern Tongues Movement Examined and Judged in the Light of the Scriptures and in the Light of its Fruits*. Long Beach, California: A.S. Pierce, 1941.

Bennett, Dennis, *Nine O'Clock in the Morning*. Plainfield, N.J.: Logos Press, 1970.

Berg, Daniel, *Enviado Por Deus, Memorias De Daniel Berg*. São Paulo: AdD, 1959.

Bruner, Frederick Dale, *A Theology of the Holy Spirit, The Pentecostal Experience and the New Testament Witness*. Grand Rapids: W.B. Eerdmans, 1970.

Carlyle, Thomas, *Reminiscences*. Edited by Charles Eliot Norton. London: MacMillan and Company, 1887.

Derstine, Gerald, *Following the Fire*. Plainfield, New Jersey: Logos International, 1980.

Dunn, James D.G., *Baptism in the Holy Spirit: A Reexamination of the New Testament Teaching of the Gift of the Spirit in Relation to Pentecostalism Today*. Napierville, Illinois: Allenson, 1970.

du Plessis, David, *A Man Called Mr. Pentecost: David du Plessis*, as told to Bob Slosser. Plainfield, New Jersey: Logos International, 1977.

Harper, Michael, *Three Sisters*. Wheaton, Illinois: Tyndale Publishers Inc., 1979.

Hoover, Willis C., *Historia del Avivamiento Pentecostal en Chile.* Valparaiso: 1948.

Ironsides, Harry A., *Holiness, The False and the True.* Neptune, New Jersey: Loizeaux Brothers, 1912.

Knapp, Martin Wells, *Lightning Bolts From Pentecostal Skies or the Devices of the Devil Unmasked.* Cincinnati: The Pentecostal Holiness Library, 1898.

Lindsell, Harold, *The Holy Spirit in the Latter Days.* Nashville: Thomas Nelson, 1983.

Mackie, Alexander, *The Gift of Tongues: A Study in the Pathological Aspect of Christianity.* New York: George H. Doran, 1921.

Mahan, Asa, *The Baptism of the Holy Ghost.* New York: W.C. Palmer, Jr., 1870.

_____, *The Scripture Doctrine of Christian Perfection.* Boston: D.S. King, 1839.

Manuel, David, *Like a Mighty River: A Personal Account of the Charismatic Conference of 1977.* Orleans, Massachussetts: Rock Harbor Press, 1977.

Martin, Ralph, *Fire on the Earth: What God Is Doing in the World Today.* Ann Arbor: Servant Books, 1975.

McDonnell, Kilian, and Arnold Bittlinger, *The Baptism in the Holy Spirit as an Ecumenical Problem.* South Bend, Indiana: Charismatic Renewal Services, 1972.

Murray, Andrew, *The Full Blessing of Pentecost.* New York: Fleming H. Revell Company, 1905.

Myland, David Wesley, *The Latter Rain Covenant and Pentecostal Power.* Chicago: Evangel Publishing House, 1910.

Roberts, Oral, *My Story.* Tulsa: privately printed, 1961.

Shakarian, Demos, *The Happiest People in the World.* Old Tappan, New Jersey: Chosen Books, 1975.

Sherrill, John, *They Speak with Other Tongues.* New York: McGraw and Hill, 1964.

Simpson, A.B., *The Holy Spirit or Power From on High.* Harrisburg, Pennsylvania: Christian Publications, Inc., 1896.

Spurgeon, Charles Haddon, *Spurgeon's Sermons.* Grand Rapids: Zondervan reprint from 1857.

Smith, Hannah Whitall, *The Christian's Secret of a Happy Life.* New York: Fleming H. Revell Company, 1870.

Stollee, H. J., *Speaking in Tongues.* Minneapolis: Augsburg Press, 1963.

Synan, Vinson, *Charismatic Bridges*. Ann Arbor: Word of Life, 1974.

Torrey, Reuben Archer, *Baptism with the Holy Spirit*. London: James Nisbet & Co. Ltd., 1895.

——————————, *The Person and the Work of the Holy Spirit*. New York: Fleming H. Revell Company, 1910.

Wagner, Peter, *Your Spiritual Gifts Can Make Your Church Grow*. Ventura, California: Regal Books, 1979.

Warfield, Benjamin B., *Counterfeit Miracles*. Carlisle, Pa.: The Banner of Truth Trust, 1918.

Wells, David, *Revolution in Rome*. Downer's Grove, Illinois: Intervarsity Press, 1972.

White, Alma, *Demons and Tongues*. Bound Brook, New Jersey: The Pentecostal Union, 1910.

Wilkerson, David, *The Cross and the Switchblade*. New York: Random House, 1963.

Secondary Sources

Anfuso, Joseph, and David Sczepanski, *He Gives, He Takes Away*. Eureka, California: Radiance Publications, 1983.

Christenson, Larry, *A Message to the Charismatic Movement*. Weymouth, Massachussetts: Dimension, 1972.

——————————, *The Charismatic Renewal among Lutherans*. Minneapolis: Lutheran Charismatic Renewal Services, 1975.

Conn, Charles W.. *Like a Mighty Army Moves the Church of God*. Cleveland, Tennessee: Church of God Publishing House, 1955.

Curtis, Richard K., *They Called Him Mr. Moody*. Garden City, New York: Doubleday & Company, 1962.

Cutten, George Bernard, *Speaking with Tongues Historically and Psychologically Considered*. New Haven: Yale University Press, 1927.

Dieter, Melvin, *The Holiness Revival of the Nineteenth Century*. Metuchen, New Jersey, 1980.

Durasoff, Steve, *Bright Wind of the Spirit*. Englewood Cliffs, N.J.: Prentice- Hall, 1972.

——————————, *Pentecost behind the Iron Curtain*. Plainfield, New Jersey: Logos International, 1972.

Harper, Michael, *As at the Beginning: The Twentieth Century Pentecostal Revival*. London: Hodder and Staughton, 1965.

Harrell, David, *All Things Are Possible: The Healing and Charismatic*

Revivals in Modern America. Bloomington, Indiana: Indiana University Press, 1975.

Hollenweger, Walter, *The Pentecostals: The Charismatic Movement in the Churches.* Minneapolis: Augsburg Press, 1972.

Kelsey, Morton, *Tongue Speaking: An Experiment in Spiritual Experience.* New York: Doubleday & Company, 1964.

Kildahl, John P., *The Psychology of Speaking in Tongues.* New York: Harper & Row, 1972.

King, Pat, *The Jesus People Are Coming.* Plainfield, New Jersey: Logos Press, 1971.

Menzies, William, *Anointed to Serve: The Story of the Assemblies of God.* Springfield, Missouri: Gospel Publishing House, 1971.

McDonnell, Kilian, *Charismatic Renewal and the Churches.* New York: The Seabury Press, 1976.

Merricks, William, *Edward Irving: The Forgotten Giant.* East Peoria, Illinois: Scribe's Chamber Publications, 1983.

Moberg, David, *The Church as a Social Institution.* Englewood Cliffs, New Jersey: Prentice-Hall, 1962.

Monterosso, Victor, William Reed, and Harman Johnson, *Latin American Church Growth.* Grand Rapids: W. B. Eerdmans, 1969.

Neibuhr, Richard, *The Social Sources of Denominationalism.* Hamden, Connecticut: The Shoestring Press, 1929.

Oates, Wayne, *Glossolalia: Tongue Speaking in Biblical, Historical, and Psychological Perspective.* Nashville: Abingdon Press, 1967.

Orr, J. Edwin, *The Flaming Tongue: The Impact of the Twentieth Century Revivals.* Chicago: Moody Press, 1973.

Parham, Sarah. E. *The Life of Charles F. Parham.* Joplin, Missouri: Tri-State Printing Company, 1930.

Plowman, Ed. *The Jesus Movement in America.* Cool, 1971.

Pope, Liston, *Millhands and Preachers: A Study of Gastonia.* New Haven: Yale University Press, 1946.

Quebedeaux, Richard, *The New Charismatics II: How a Christian Renewal Movement Became Part of the American Religious Mainstream.* San Francisco: Harper & Row Publishers, 1983.

Ranaghan, Kevin and Dorothy, *Catholic Pentecostals.* Paramus, New Jersey: Paulist Press, 1969.

Rifkin, Jeremy, with Ted Howard, *The Emerging Order: God in the Age of Scarcity.* New Yord: G.P. Putnam's Sons, 1979.

Root, Jean Christie, *Edward Irving: Man, Preacher, Prophet.* Boston: Sherman, French & Company, 1912.

Sandeen, Ernest, *The Roots of Fundamentalism: British and American Millenarianism.* 1800-1930. Chicago: University of Chicago Press, 1970.

Smith, Timothy, *Called Unto Holiness.* Kansas City: Nazarene Publishing House, 1962.

——————————, *Revivalism and Social Reform in Mid-Nineteenth Century America.* New York: Abingdon Press, 1957.

Spittler, Russell, *Perspectives on the New Pentecostalism.* Grand Rapids, Michigan: Baker Book House, 1976

Strachan, Gordon, *The Pentecostal Theology of Edward Irving.* London: Dartan, Longman & Todd, 1973.

Sullivan, Francis, S.J., *Charisms and Charismatic Renewal.* Ann Arbor: Servant Books, 1982.

Synan, Vinson, Ed., *Aspects of Pentecostal-Charismatic Origins.* Plainfield, New Jersey: Logos International, 1975.

——————————, *The Holiness-Pentecostal Movement in the United States.* Grand Rapids: Wm. B. Eerdmans, 1972.

——————————, *The Old-Time Power: A History of the Pentecostal Holiness Church.* Franklin Springs, Georgia: Advocate Press, 1973.

Vergara, Ignacio, *El Protestantismo En Chile.* Santiago: 1962.

Wagner, Peter, *Look Out, The Pentecostals Are Coming.* Carol Stream, Illinois: Creation House, 1973.

Wood, William W., *Culture and Personality Aspects of the Pentecostal Holiness Religion.* The Hague: Mouton Company, 1965.

Articles

Bresee, Phineas, "The Gift of Tongues," *The Nazarene Messenger,* December 13, 1906, p. 6.

du Plessis, David, "Newsletter" (February-March), 1984.

Farrell, Frank, "Outburst of Tongues: The New Penetration," *Christianity Today* 7 (September 13, 1963), pp. 3-7.

Flower, J. Roswell, "Birth of the Pentecostal Movement," *The Pentecostal Evangel* (November 26, 1950), p. 3.

Gray, Paul, "Six Years Later," *New Covenant* 8 (February, 1973).

Hughes, Ray, "A Traditional Pentecostal Looks at the New Pentecostals," *Christianity Today* 18 (June 7, 1974), pp. 6-10.

Kantzer, Kenneth, "The Charismatics Among Us," *Christianity Today* 24 (February 22, 1980), pp. 25-29.

Lindsell, Harold, "My Search For the Truth About the Holy Spirit," *Christian Life* (September, 1983), p. 29.

Mac Collam, Joel A., "O Lord, We're Free at Last," *Charisma* (October, 1983), pp. 40-46.

Ostling, Richard, "Counting Every Soul on Earth," *Time* (May 3, 1982), pp. 66-67.

Rose, Bruce L., "Episcopal Church: Catholic-Evangelical-Charismatic," *Acts* 29 (February, 1984), pp. 1-6.

Stump, David X., "Charismatic Renewal: Up to Date in Kansas City," *America* (September 24, 1977).

Sydnor, Charles Jr., "The Pentecostals," *Presbyterian Survey* (May, 1964), 36-39.

Synan, Vinson, "The World's Largest Congregation: A Cathedral in Chile," *Christianity Today* 19 (January 17, 1975), pp. 33-34.

Towns, Elmer, "The World's Ten Largest Churches," *Christian Life* (January, 1983), pp. 60-66.

Van Dusen, Henry P., "Third Force in Christendom," *Life* (June 9, 1958), pp. 113-124.

Wagner, Peter, "A Third Wave?" *Pastoral Renewal* 8 (July-August, 1983), 1-5.

Willoughby, Williams, "Tongues Speaking Gains Prestige," *Logos* (April, 1974), pp. 59-60.

Collections, Minutes, and Unpublished Materials

Barrett, David, *The World Christian Encyclopedia*. New York: Oxford University Press, 1982.

Jacquet, Constance, *Yearbook of American and Canadian Churches*. Nashville: Abingdon Press, 1983.

Jones, Charles, *A Guide to the Study of the Pentecostal Movement*. Metuchen, New Jersey: The Scarecrow Press, 1974.

_____, *A Guide to the Study of the Pentecostal Movement*. 3 vols. Metuchen, New Jersey: The Scarecrow Press, 1983.

Lewis, Warren, *Witnesses to the Holy Spirit*. Valley Forge, Pennsylvania: Judson Press, 1978.

McDonnell, Kilian, *Presence, Power, Praise: Documents on the Charismatic Renewal*. 3 vols. Collegeville, Minnesota: Liturgical Press, 1980.

Schaff, Philip, *Nicene and Post-Nicene Fathers*, vol. 12. Grand Rapids: Wm. B. Eerdmans Publishing Company, 1956.

Personal Interviews with the Author

The author interviewed the following people for this book: Dennis Bennett, Johnny Bartleman, Reinhard Bonnke, Pat Boone, Brick Bradford, Larry Christenson, Paul Yongii Cho, Ithiel Clemmons, Charles W. Conn, Donald Dayton, Gerald Derstine, Melvin Dieter, David du Plessis, Steve Durasoff, Howard Ervin, J. Roswell Flower, Donald Gee, Bert Ghezzi, Michael Harper, David Harrell, Walter Hollenweger, Mario Hoover, Ray Hughes, Charles E. Jones.

Also: Klaud Kendrick, Bob Mumford, Lewi Pethrus, Kevin Ranaghan, Ralph Martin, Kilian McDonnell, William W. Menzies, Efrain Rios Montt, Edward O'Connor, Richard Ostling, Pauline Parham, J.O. Patterson, Oral Roberts, Ernest Sandeen, Demos Shakarian, Charles Simpson, Timothy Smith, Leon Joseph Cardinal Suenens, Joseph A. Synan, Milton Tomlinson, Nathaniel Urshan, Javier Vasquez, Peter Wagner, David Wilkerson, Peter Varonaev.

Index